Readers are aware that the Joyce 'oeuvre' is haunted by ghosts, shades, elusive and allusive fleeting asides, heaps of broken images where the 'sun beats and the dead tree gives no shelter'. The bitterness of usurpation and betrayal stalks his pages, and to the dismay of many a reader, emotional passion can be obscured by his 'catalectic tetrameter(s) of iambs marching'. But what or who haunts this vast oeuvre of James Joyce?

Mary Adams unlocks the puzzle of the haunting in her theorising of 'the replacement child'. She illuminates the harsh and lyrical linguistic landscape of Finnegans Wake, decompressing and revealing huge emotional intensity on the page. Reminding us that the unconscious is in the language not behind it!

Adams gives us a deeply poignant and vivid portrait of the man, his family, his work and his world, and gives a voice to the silence around the death of Joyce's 'firstborn sibling'. She is a gifted psychoanalyst with a deep understanding of the poetry of dreams showing us how they catch and give formal representation to our passions. Her analysis gives us a heartfelt full-blooded picture of Joyce the man, the artist and genius.

Dr Paul Caviston FRCPsych

Mary Adams' book is a work of Joycean scholarship, worn admirably lightly. Her love of James Joyce and his work illuminates the text. At the same time, it is a wonderfully concise, yet deeply thoughtful and moving exposition of the psychoanalytic and philosophical concepts which shape the replacement child's internal world. The book will be of interest to analysts, child psychotherapists and lovers of James Joyce.

Hilary Lester, *Training Analyst for the Society of Analytical Psychology*

In the author's view, James Joyce is one of a surprising number of gifted writers and artists – Rilke and Van Gogh are others – who were born as 'replacement babies' to mothers who had lost a previous child. Drawing on her experience as a psychoanalyst, Mary Adams gives a subtle, admiring and scholarly account of Joyce's life and work. She interprets it as his lifelong response to the painful beginning of his life and its unconscious meanings for him. Present in his work are not only memories of his family, but also of the multitude who were abandoned to die in the Irish Famine. This succinct book will encourage readers to return to Joyce's great writings with an enriched interest.

Michael Rustin, *Professor of Sociology, Associate of the British Psychoanalytical Society*

T0349761

I found this book captivating and very moving. The seamless movement between Joyce the lived experience, patients and psychoanalytic texts brings each to life in a way that emphasises their connectedness, which in turn is reflected in the quality and sensitivity of the writing. I felt I learnt much about the ubiquity of psychic pain and the efforts to mitigate it.

Julian Lousada, *British Psychoanalytic Association*

James Joyce and the Internal World of the Replacement Child

This book is an exploration of the internal world of James Joyce with particular emphasis on his being born into his parents' grief at the loss of their firstborn son, offering a new perspective on his emotional difficulties.

Mary Adams links Joyce's profound sense of guilt and abandonment with the trauma of being a 'replacement child' and compares his experience with that of two psychoanalytic cases, as well as with Freud and other well-known figures who were replacement children. Issues such as survivor guilt, sibling rivalry, the 'illegitimate' replacement son and the 'dead mother' syndrome are discussed. Joyce is seen as maturing from a paranoid, fearful state through his writing, his intelligence, his humour and his sublime poetic sensibility. By escaping the oppressive aspects of life in Dublin, in exile he could find greater emotional freedom and a new sense of belonging. A quality of claustrophobic intrusive identification in *Ulysses* contrasts strikingly with a new levity, imaginative identification, intimacy and compassion in *Finnegans Wake*. *James Joyce and the Internal World of the Replacement Child* highlights the concept of the replacement child and the impact this can have on a whole family.

The book will be of interest to psychoanalysts, psychoanalytic psychotherapists and child psychotherapists as well as students of English literature, psychoanalytic studies and readers interested in James Joyce.

Mary Adams is a psychoanalyst working in London. She is a member of the British Psychoanalytic Association and was a training analyst for the Association of Child Psychotherapists. She worked as a psychiatric social worker in London and Boston (USA). She was the Editor of *The Journal of the British Association of Psychotherapists* (1999–2005).

Routledge Focus on Mental Health

Routledge Focus on Mental Health presents short books on current topics, linking in with cutting-edge research and practice.

Titles in the series:

Working with Interpreters in Psychological Therapy
The Right to be Understood
Jude Boyles and Nathalie Talbot

Psychoanalysis and Euripides' Suppliant Women
A Tragic Reading of Politics
Sotiris Manolopoulos

The Gifts We Receive from Animals
Stories to Warm the Heart
Lori R. Kogan

James Joyce and the Internal World of the Replacement Child
Mary Adams

Analytic Listening in Clinical Dialogue
Basic Assumptions
Dieter Bürgin, Angelika Staehle, Kerstin Westhoff, and Anna Wyler von Ballmoos

Treatment for Body-Focused Repetitive Behaviors
An Integrative Psychodynamic Approach
Stacy K. Nakell

For a full list of titles in this series, please visit https://www.routledge.com/Routledge-Focus-on-Mental-Health/book-series/RFMH

James Joyce and the Internal World of the Replacement Child

Mary Adams

LONDON AND NEW YORK

First published 2023
by Routledge
4 Park Square, Milton Park, Abingdon, Oxon OX14 4RN

and by Routledge
605 Third Avenue, New York, NY 10158

Routledge is an imprint of the Taylor & Francis Group, an informa business

© 2023 Mary Adams

The right of Mary Adams to be identified as author of this work
has been asserted in accordance with sections 77 and 78 of the
Copyright, Designs and Patents Act 1988.

Trademark notice: Product or corporate names may be trademarks
or registered trademarks, and are used only for identification and
explanation without intent to infringe.

British Library Cataloguing-in-Publication Data
A catalogue record for this book is available from the British Library

Library of Congress Cataloging-in-Publication Data
Names: Adams, Mary (Psychoanalyst), author.
Title: James Joyce and the internal world of the replacement child /
Mary Adams.
Description: First edition. | Abingdon, Oxon ; New York :
Routledge, 2023 |
Series: Routledge focus on mental health | Includes bibliographical
references and index.
Identifiers: LCCN 2022012828 | ISBN 9781032314754 (hardback) |
ISBN 9781032314778 (paperback) | ISBN 9781003309925 (ebook)
Subjects: LCSH: Joyce, James, 1882-1941—Mental health. |
Novelists, Irish—20th century—Family relationships. | Novelists,
English—20th century—Biography. | Literature and mental illness. |
Men—Mental health.
Classification: LCC PR6019.O9 Z5227 2023 | DDC 823/.912 [B]—dc21
LC record available at https://lccn.loc.gov/2022012828

ISBN: 978-1-032-31475-4 (hbk)
ISBN: 978-1-032-31477-8 (pbk)
ISBN: 978-1-003-30992-5 (ebk)

DOI: 10.4324/9781003309925

Typeset in Bembo
by codeMantra

Contents

Figure

Foreword

James Joyce appeared in my life eight years ago, like a 'replacement', shortly after my husband, James Fisher, died. A psychoanalyst like myself, James endured uncomplainingly a 20-year illness, immersing himself in his work and his writing, as did Joyce. We had plans to collaborate, using his writing on the imagination and my clinical material, and since his death I have tried to continue this.

When in 2014 I signed up for a course on *Ulysses*, taught by the ever-inspiring Toby Brothers of the London Literary Salon, I felt lost in the grief that pervades the book. I was drawn to 'Buck Mulligan', who seemed a strong and lively presence for Joyce, reminding me of my psychoanalyst, Anton Obholzer. Reading about Joyce, I saw striking similarities between him and my patients who had lost siblings in childhood. On discovering that Joyce's parents had lost their first son, my direction for this book was set.

I first presented my ideas about Joyce at a Tavistock Centre Meltzer conference, to an audience who were missing my husband, James. Like a replacement child, I felt the confusion of the usurper and interloper. I joined an all-Irish James Joyce reading group and was amusingly given 'probationary' status, only to discover soon after that my great grandmother came from County Cork. When I later presented my work to a group at the Birmingham Trust for Psychoanalytic Psychotherapy, led by Kevin Booth, they responded enthusiastically. I also had RSC actor, Patrick Drury, generously join me for a presentation in which he, beautifully, read from *Ulysses*.

After six years, I married my widowed friend, Peter Loose. We honeymooned in Dublin, visited the Martello Tower and memorably joined others in Sweny's Pharmacy to read aloud from the moving last pages of *Finnegans Wake*. 'So soft this morning, ours'!

It is always a privilege when patients enter into the dialogue that is psychoanalysis. It was also a privilege to have known Donald Meltzer, personally and through his writing. Both he and the work of the child psychotherapists remain a great inspiration. Donald Meltzer and James Joyce, with their brilliant minds, difficult lives, yet revolutionary work had, I believe, much in common, not least their humanity.

My thanks go to friends and colleagues who have supported me and encouraged my writing, including especially: Joy Matthews, Colin and Jo Adams, Hilary Lester, Helen Taylor Robinson, Paul Caviston, Maureen Diffley, David Black, Juliet Newbigin, Joey Horsley, Luise Pusch, Dorothy Judd, Moira Doolan, Philip Hewitt, Martin Kemp, Eliana Pinto, Viveka Nyberg, Alan Horrox, Maggie and Rob Schaedel, Alberto Hahn, Michael and Margaret Rustin, Julian Lousada, Noel Hess, Lynne Scrimshaw, Georgie Hardie, Stephen Robertson, Davor Tovarlaza, Sanda Pajic, Harriet Berry, Simon Bergin, Shirley and Andrew Philips, Jan and Ray Derry.

My special thanks go also to the NHS Royal Free Hospital Scleroderma team and their brilliant (Irish) doctor, Niamh Quillinan, who supported me through James' illness. Dublin poet, Louise C. Callaghan introduced me to her city and to the Wicklow Mountains. And Dublin journalist, Tom Cleary, keeps me in touch with the town that 'wanders between hill and sea', sending photos of the sunset 'soft and crimson-flecked' water of the 'forty-foot'—Joyce and Gogarty's bathing spot.

For my parents, Barbara and Laurence, Joyce would have been their kind of hero. Now I am blessed to be with Peter, an irreverent classicist and companion. Peter's children, Julian and Helen, and their families have welcomed me, giving me, like Joyce, a new sense of belonging. As I come to the end of this gift of a Joycean episode in my life, it is to Peter, and to Jim, and to James Joyce that, as Anthony Burgess put it, 'my heart bows down'.

Mary Adams

Note on texts

The following abbreviations and editions have been used:

U James Joyce (1960/80). *Ulysses*, The Bodley Head.

FW James Joyce (2012). *Finnegans Wake*, Oxford World Classics, OUP.

D James Joyce (2000). *Dubliners*, Penguin Classics.

P James Joyce (2000a). *Portrait of the Artist as a Young Man*, Penguin Modern Classics.

OCPW James Joyce (2000). *Occasional, Critical, and Political Writing*, ed. Kevin Barry, Oxford.

SL James Joyce, *Selected Letters*, Richard Ellmann, editor (1992), Faber & Faber.

JJ Richard Ellmann (1982). *James Joyce*, revised edition, Oxford.

Acknowledgements

Mary Adams

I would like to thank Trinity College Dublin for permission to reproduce the *Chi Rho* from the *Book of Kells*, and Cambridge University Press for permission to quote from J. Whitebook, *Freud. An Intellectual Biography*, and *The Cambridge Companion to James Joyce*.

Introduction

'First born, first fruit of woe'
'A hundred cares, a tithe of troubles and is there one who understands me?'
[FW]

This book is an exploration of the internal world of James Joyce and the question, 'why was he so troubled in life?' I link his profound sense of guilt and abandonment with the trauma of being a 'replacement child' after the death of a sibling. While his childhood was difficult in many ways, I believe his parents' loss of their firstborn son, although not spoken about, significantly affected him and contributed to his life-long feeling marginalised and 'exiled in on himself'. His parents viewed Joyce as a special child because he was exceptionally bright but also, no doubt, because their first child who had been eagerly anticipated had died a year before in 1881. Joyce would have been born while his parents were still grieving. He was described as a sensitive child with an active imagination and phenomenal memory who absorbed everything around him. He never spoke openly of his parents' first loss but *Ulysses* revolves around a couple, Molly and Bloom, whose lives were blighted by the loss of their firstborn son and Stephen Dedalus refers to himself as a changeling, split between 'the true Irish son and the fraudulent outsider'.
    I follow Joyce's emotional development from the troubled but brilliant, swashbuckling, arrogant teenager whose early polemic 'rings with a steely authority, urbanity flung like a careless cloak across a murderous sword' (Flanagan, 1975), to the grieving, intrusive (verging on the pornographic) lonely author of *Ulysses*, to, ultimately, the humane, revolutionary, heart-stopping poet of *Finnegans Wake*. Joyce's writing is autobiographical and conveys, at one level, considerable early pain. 'My youth was exceptionally violent; painful and violent', he told his close friend, Arthur Power.

DOI: 10.4324/9781003309925-1

I found striking similarities between Joyce and two of my psychoanalytic patients who lost siblings in childhood. There is a general silence about the 'replacement child' and my patients initially dismissed the idea as having no significance, but we came to see how pervasive the effects can be. They were both intelligent, talented adults but had always felt to blame for their mother's grief and were convinced they could cause damage or even death to others. It had become a fixed delusional belief. 'You say I *think* I am lethal', said one patient, 'but I *know* I am'. They were both in their 40s but crippled by constant nightmares of monsters and dead babies. Like Joyce, they were living in exile and always felt on the margins. They were full of fear, saw no way out, became suicidal and turned to drink.

James Joyce lived all his life in a similar fearful state. He had disabling phobias and he, too, was plagued by nightmares. He spoke of 'that skull' that came to torment him at night. In a letter, he wrote: 'Can you tell me what is a cure for dreaming? I am troubled every night by horrible and terrifying dreams: death, corpses, assassinations in which I take an unpleasantly prominent part'. Writing held him together but he described being 'a paper leaf away from madness' and at times turned to alcohol.

The 2020 Nobel prize winner, poet Louise Glück, wrote a poem, 'Lost love' which alludes to the sister who died before she was born: 'Her death was not my experience, but her absence was' (Chiasson, 2012). I believe the 'absence' of Joyce's brother, the first born, remained very present. Joyce's mother had several miscarriages and Joyce rails against the constant pregnancies which occupied her and wore her down. But particularly powerful would have been awareness of her lost firstborn—expressed early in his writing, perhaps, by the wife, Gretta in *The Dead,* grieving for her 'first love' who had died, 'a young boy... very delicate' (*D*, p. 220). Joyce's father, devastated at the loss, said it was never to be mentioned. The father increasingly turned to alcohol and one wonders how much the loss contributed to his decline.

As well as Glück's poetry, we have the playwright David Storey's (2021) harrowing memoir, addressed throughout to the brother who died, at age 6, while Storey was still in the womb. His daily struggle, sense of terror and need to immerse himself in writing, echoes Joyce's life.

Although he was special to both parents, Joyce felt himself an outsider—a feeling common in replacement children. This sense of dis-location is echoed in *Portrait of an Artist*, where he says about Stephen:

> To merge his life in the common tide of other lives was harder for him than any fasting or prayer ... He saw clearly ... his own futile isolation. He had not ... bridged the restless shame and rancour that had divided him from mother and brother and sister. He felt that

he was hardly of the one blood with them but stood to them rather in the mystical kinship of fosterage, foster child and foster brother.

(*P*, p. 105)

Survivor guilt in the replacement child can leave them feeling they have no right to belong, that they are sentenced to a life of exile. Joyce lived all his adult life in exile and identified with Dante, as though banished from Ireland. I explore the self-banishment of the replacement child. Survivor guilt can also produce a paranoid inner world, reminiscent of the claustrum described by Donald Meltzer. Joyce gives a brilliant portrayal of a Kafkaesque persecutory state of mind in his *Circe* court-room scene in *Ulysses* which has all the pathos, illogic, desperate hilarity and 'no way out'. It foreshadows *Finnegans Wake*, showing Joyce's own struggle with 'who to blame' and his genius at dramatizing it. It begins:

Georges Fottrell (Clerk of the crown and peace, resonantly): Order in court!

The accused will now make a bogus statement. (Bloom, pleading not guilty and holding a full blown water lily, begins a long unintelligible speech…)

(U 587)

The pervasive sense of guilt of the replacement child is, against any logic or evidence, played out in *Ulysses* in all its sadness. In *Finnegans Wake*, however, while issues of guilt and blame still dominate, there is a shift in mood and a freedom from persecution. There is much gossip and rivalry and assumed sexual transgression, but no evidence of serious crime is found. There are twin brothers, Shem and Shaun, (Joyce and the lost brother?) and brotherly rivalry, but this is resolved:

We're as thick and thin now as two tubular jawballs. I hate him about his patent henesy, pfasfh it, yet am I amorist. I love him. I love his old portugal's nose.

(FW, 463.18)

The wife in *Finnegans Wake* writes her famous letter to excuse her husband's wrongdoing. She implies the letter is *Finnegans Wake* itself trying to be an apology and says it is hard to fathom: 'Every letter is a hard but yours sure is the hardest crux ever'.

Joyce could recognise the guilt instilled in him by the Catholic church and by his denial of his mother's wishes but he sensed there was something deeper at play, something which I am describing as survivor guilt. One patient of mine, full of inexplicable feelings of guilt, on hearing an ex-prisoner say 'how can I make a life for myself when I have murdered someone', said 'I know what he means'. She could hear how absurd that was but she still felt convinced she had caused a death—presumably the death of the sister who died *before she was born*.

A silent backdrop to Joyce's writing is the 1845–1852 Irish Famine. Like the loss of his parents' firstborn, the Famine, which had devastated Ireland only 30 years before Joyce was born, could not be spoken about. His father was born during the Famine in County Cork which experienced the worst losses. The trauma which paralysed Ireland has parallels with the experience of the replacement child who is left feeling to blame for the tragedy which devastated his family. Some critics, like Eagleton, were asking 'where is the Famine in Joyce's writing?' (Toibin and Ferriter, 2001), but more recently *Ulysses* has been described as a brilliant fable exposing Ireland's complicity in the devastation (Roos, 2005).

It is extraordinary how Joyce writes his emotional struggle so beguilingly onto the page. His wife, Nora, said she would hear him chuckling to himself as he wrote *Finnegans Wake* late at night and it clearly kept him sane. But it is also tragic to picture someone working so assiduously all his life to try to assuage a guilt that could not be identified. Joyce argued that emotional, not intellectual, factors propelled his writing:

> Emotion has dictated the course and detail of my book, and in emotional writing one arrives at the unpredictable which can be of more value, since its sources are deeper, than the products of the intellectual method.
>
> (Norris, 2011, p. 156)

This comment is key and conveys a hope that he may understand his fears by writing. At the same time, his extraordinary play with language was an attempt to obscure emotion in what he wrote, as though afraid of what was emerging. The renowned literary critic, Harry Levin, taken aback by Joyce's obscuring emotion said, 'The nearer Joyce comes to a scene or an emotion, the more prone he is to indulge in literary by-play' (1944, p. 161). As Devlin describes,

> Language is put through a smeltingworks forever decomposed and recomposed. Broken down into bits that are then fused or 'coupled' into new elements, the words in the *Wake* are subjected to a process somewhat similar to the stewing of the relics in the midden:

'a bone, a pebble, a ramskin; chip them, chap them, cut them up allways; leave them to terracook in the muttheringpot'.

[FW 20] (1991, p. 12)

James Fisher, in discussing Bion and the fear of emotion, wrote:

As Bion emphasized numerous times, it is the hatred of emotion that lies at the heart of psychotic phenomena. Paradoxically certain emotions, such as anxiety, envy and hatred, attack and make impossible the experiencing of other emotions. Actually, rather than envy, perhaps we should put fear at the head of the list of minus K factors, the fear that emotional experience is not survivable.

(2006, p. 1233)

Joyce was full of fear but he was a passionate man and his writing is full of emotion. Particularly shocking was the fury (and longing) expressed towards their mothers by Joyce and my two patients. The mother who loses a child is often experienced as turning away from the family and, in her grief, becoming the 'dead mother', emotionally unavailable. *Ulysses* is full of grief but also rage at the mother. Stephen, haunted by a nightmare of his dead mother returning to reproach him, cries out: 'Ghoul! Chewer of corpses!' and then pleads with her, 'No, mother. Let me be and let me live' He speaks of her 'hardness of heart', 'black basilisk eyes with the power to poison', a 'withering mind', her 'cold blighted love for him'. '…thou has suckled me with a bitter milk; my moon and my sun thou has quenched forever'

The extended hallucinatory *Circe* episode of *Ulysses* immediately follows *Oxen of the Sun* which takes place in the maternity hospital where Mrs Purefoy is giving birth to 'yet another baby'—her ninth of twelve. Not only is it as though writing about this birth of a baby boy touched on traumatic memories and produced this new outpouring in Joyce, which he called, 'a vision animated to bursting point', but *Circe* ends with an image of Bloom's lost baby son.

Some of the writers with whom Joyce felt a strong affinity had also lost siblings in childhood, namely, Shakespeare, Milton, Blake, Ibsen and Freud. I look at Shakespeare's plea to his abandoning mother after she lost three daughters and at Freud's struggle with his mother after the death of his brother. Joyce seems to play out his confusion over 'who is to blame' in his discussion of Shakespeare and Hamlet in *Ulysses*. As discussed by Janet Adelman, mothers and their sexuality are a powerful target of rage in the abandoned son. In Shakespeare, there are no mothers in nine of his plays, and Freud, like Joyce, blocked any mention of his own mother. In psychoanalysis, it took Melanie Klein to bring the focus onto the mother. One wonders whether Freud and Breuer, who both lost siblings in childhood, would still have labelled 'Anna O' a hysteric if they had focussed on her early sibling loss rather than Oedipal issues. Their discussions are reminiscent of psychiatrists diagnosing mental illness in women while ignoring the fact that they had been sexually abused. Similarly, neither Freud nor Ernest Jones, who both saw Joan Riviere in analysis, focussed on the fact that her parents lost a newborn son just a year before she was born.

Central in the internal world of the replacement child is the child's imagination. As described by Melanie Klein, children have murderous phantasies towards mother's other babies. If these phantasies coincide with the actual death of a sibling, the child fears that wishes can become reality just by thinking them. In the psychoanalytic literature, there are poignant accounts of patients who felt they actually caused or should have prevented the sibling's death even though, like Joyce, they had not yet been born.

The famous beginning in *Ulysses,* set in the claustrum-like Martello Tower, dramatically encapsulates the world of the replacement child with its rivalry between brothers and accusations of guilt. In Chapter 8, I look at the intense relationship between Joyce and Oliver St John Gogarty, the model for 'Buck Mulligan' and with whom he stayed in the Martello Tower. Gogarty, a popular Dublin poet and senator, who remained at the centre of life in Dublin, could be seen as Joyce's lost older brother—the 'legitimate' one who haunts him all his life.

My replacement child patients and Joyce all tried to escape their sense of not belonging by going into exile but they were still persecuted by their imagination and nightmares. They had techniques for controlling their inner turmoil in their waking state, adopting, for example, a proleptic imagination, but they could not control their dreams. A proleptic imagination gives a false security that we *know* what will happen, but if the underlying belief is that we will be exposed and condemned, we are left waiting in dread, unable to imagine things differently. With *Ulysses,* Joyce portrays Stephen condemned for denying his mother's dying wishes. He is then caught in a world of blame, unable to intimately engage with anyone. It is a study of isolation and announces to the world that he is this bad person. Ironically, the years of legal debate over whether *Ulysses* should be published, and his notoriety for exploiting others for financial and other kinds of support seems to play out for Joyce discussion of his badness for all the world to see. It is as though actually becoming bad can paradoxically offer the replacement child an authentic self and a rightful place to be.

I look at Joyce's attempts to control his active imagination by channelling it into his writing. As discussed by Coleridge and, more recently, by the psychoanalyst, Thomas Ogden, the distinction between controlled fantasy and a free imagination is paramount. While Joyce's writing seems like a free imagination gone wild, in reality it is carefully controlled. His phenomenal memory allowed him to fill his books with real events and real facts. As Wyndham Lewis put it, '*Ulysses* confines the reader in a circumscribed psychological space into which several encyclopaedias have been emptied' (1927, p. 91). However, having a phenomenal memory can hinder the need to let go of painful images. It may give the illusion of control, but it also produces an isolating omniscience. Growing up, James Joyce, 'the injustice collector', became full of resentment at his world, remembering every slight and feeling increasingly persecuted. However, although he disparaged psychoanalysis for himself, he seems to have used his writing to articulate and slowly distance himself from the memories, as one does in psychoanalysis. It is impressive to see the transformation in him and how he 'mellowed'. Perhaps, by placing *Finnegans Wake* in the night time dreamworld, Joyce had found a way to control the dreams that plagued him. His friend, Gerald Griffin, describes the change in him:

> That is Joyce as he is now—tolerant of all criticism, confident that he is right, yet sensitive to the last degree. The truculent, almost swashbuckling, hard-swearing, seedy-looking young Dubliner has merged into the mellow, genial, quiet, well-dressed man of poise and distinction. Aloof and frigid to gate-crashing journalists, he is the soul of hospitality and generosity to his personal friends.
>
> (1990, p. 153)

In his 17-year immersion writing *Finnegans Wake*, it is as though Joyce's self-reproach and reproach towards Ireland become externalised into his characters where the guilt can be mocked, puzzled over and ultimately forgiven. This is a striking developmental shift in Joyce. In *Ulysses,* there is no forgiveness. As John Banville asks: 'What happened to Joyce in those *Wanderjahre*? How was the precious young man who had set out to "forge the conscience of my race" enabled to find within himself that tremendous humanistic and comic gift?' (1999).

In *Finnegans Wake,* HCE, the husband/father, is accused but no serious evidence of guilt is found and the wife, Anna Livia, caringly explains and defends him. Described as a 'puntomime', Joyce's imagination now has the freedom of the dreamworld. I suggest that in moving from the imprisoning, persecuting nightmare of *Ulysses* into the dreamworld of

Finnegans Wake it is like dreamwork in psychoanalysis, for which the patient steps outside himself.

It is not clear whether Joyce's nightmares continued all his life, but perhaps locating *Finnegans Wake* in the world of the dream was an attempt to take control of them. His intense involvement in writing *Finnegans Wake*, often late into the night, could be Joyce trying to get the better of his own internal world—he would craft his own dreams! A link is made with Shakespeare's late play, *The Winter's Tale*, with the dream sequence in Bohemia leading to a waking of the 'dead mother' statue of Hermione.

Although still obsessive in his attempts to obscure emotion, what emerges is a new depressive position sense of emotional intimacy and connection with the world. As in all of Joyce's writing, we are still in Dublin, but now there is a family at the centre and a sense of belonging. The issue of belonging winds its way through Joyce's life. The replacement child can feel there is no place for them in their parents' eyes, or that they do not deserve to belong in the family when their sibling had died.

This differs from the kinds of discrimination other children experience in the sense that for the replacement child there has been a death in the family. Other children will have murderous feelings towards siblings, daughters may resent sons being favoured and feel unseen, for example, but the devastating issue here is the fear and confusion in the child when murderous fantasy becomes reality and the mother suddenly turns to stone.

It is my hope that by linking the internal world of James Joyce with the 'dead mother' syndrome and the trauma of sibling loss, clinical practitioners may more readily consider the fate of the replacement child as well as recognising the problems of having a phenomenal memory, the reality of transgenerational trauma, the trap of a proleptic imagination and the use of intrusive, as opposed to imaginative, identification. My patients' lives were transformed and their nightmares ceased when they could see how much they were still affected by unconscious fears in relation to their own sibling loss. It is my sense that much pain and fear could be lifted if patients were helped to believe that childhood rivalrous wishes are universal and not the cause of sibling deaths.

Phillippe Soupault, paying tribute to Joyce on his 50th birthday wrote:

> Joyce's friends, more comprehending, are thinking of his health, of his sadness. And joining with them, I come to him strong in my friendship, and in the respectful and intimate affection which binds me to this unclassifiable man, to this man who is strong in his

weakness, to this great writer who is, first of all, a man who suffers and smiles. Behind him move, as though against a stage curtain, the shadows of Dedalus, of Bloom, and of Anna Livia.

(1990, p. 141)

References

Adelman, J. (1992). *Suffocating Mothers: Fantasies of Maternal Origin in Shakespeare's Plays, Hamlet to The Tempest*. London: Routledge.

Banville, J. (1999). The Motherless Child. *New York Review of Books*, December 16.

Chiasson, D. (2012). The Body Artist. Louise Glueck's Collected Poems. *The New Yorker*, November 4.

Devlin, K. J. (1991) *Wandering and Return in Finnegans Wake: An Integrative Approach to Joyce's Fictions*. Princeton, NJ: Princeton Legacy Library, PUP.

Fisher, J. V. (2006). The Emotional Experience of K, *The International Journal of Psychoanalysis*, 87: 1221–1237.

Flanagan, T. (1975). 'Yeats, Joyce and Ireland', in *Critical Inquiry*. Chicago, IL: U Chicago P, pp. 43–67.

Griffin, G. (1990). 'James Joyce', in E. H. Mikhail, ed., *James Joyce. Interviews and Recollections*. London: Macmillan Press.

Joyce, J. (2000). *Dubliners*. London: Penguin Classics.

Joyce, J. (2000a). *Portrait of the Artist as a Young Man*. London: Penguin Modern Classics.

Levin, H. (1960). *James Joyce*. London: New Directions.

Lewis, W. (1927). *Time and Western Man*, Chapter XVI: 'An Analysis of the mind of James Joyce'. London: Chatto & Windus.

Norris, M. (2011). 'Finnegans Wake', in D. Attridge, ed., *Cambridge Companion to James Joyce*. 2nd ed. Cambridge: Cambridge UP, pp. 149–171.

Roos, B. (2005). 'The Joyce of Eating: Feast, Famine and the Humble Potato in *Ulysses*', in G. Cusack & S. Goss, eds., *Hungry Words. Images of Famine in the Irish Canon*. Dublin: Irish Academic Press, pp. 159–196.

Soupault, P. in Mikhail, E. H. ed. (1990). *James Joyce: Interviews and Recollections*. London: Macmillan Press, pp. 141–143.

Storey, D. (2021). *A Stinging Delight. David Story: A Memoir*. London: Faber & Faber.

Toibin, C., & Ferriter, D. (2001). *The Irish Famine. A Documentary*. New York: St Martin's Press.

1 *Freud*. His lost brother and 'dead mother'

I begin by comparing James Joyce with his contemporary, Sigmund Freud. For both, their earliest experience was blighted by their mother's grief at the death of their brother. They both struggled with considerable guilt including survivor guilt, guilt for having murderous wishes towards siblings and believing they caused their mother's grief. Trying to understand himself and his nightmares, Joyce studied Freud closely, especially *The Interpretation of Dreams*, but neither he nor Freud could give full importance to their earliest experience. Freud, writing near the end of his life, implies how much the infantile trauma was repressed:

> Everything in the sphere of this first attachment to the mother seemed to me so difficult to grasp in analysis—so grey with age and shadowy and almost impossible to revivify—that it was as if it had succumbed to an especially inexorable repression.
>
> (Freud, 1931, p. 226)

Freud was only one year old when his brother, Julius, was born and died six months later, making Freud, like James Joyce, in the broad sense, a 'replacement child', the survivor/usurper. Freud's family lived in a one-room apartment so he would have been exposed at first hand to his brother's illness and perhaps even to his death (Schur, 1972, 241). In a letter to Fliess, he wrote, 'I welcomed my one-year-younger brother (who died within a few months) with ill wishes and real infantile jealousy, and his death left the germ of guilt in me' (Schur, 1969, p. 305). Among his earliest memories were guilt feelings and the fulfilment of his death wishes towards Julius aroused in him a lifelong tendency toward self-reproach. James Hamilton links this to Freud's thinking about the death instinct:

> Freud commented at length on the significance of death wishes and the loss of siblings in 'The Interpretation of Dreams' (1900):

DOI: 10.4324/9781003309925-2

'Deaths that are experienced in this way in childhood may quickly be forgotten in the family; but psychoanalytic research shows that they have a very important influence on subsequent neuroses'. In Freud's case the failure to have worked through the loss of Julius, burdened him with intense survivor guilt and fear of retaliation which, in turn would account for his constant, almost daily, preoccupation with death.

(1976, p. 150)

Freud was at a disadvantage analysing himself as so much of one's infancy is inaccessible. He did not have the benefit of Melanie Klein's descriptions of the internal world of young children, which could have reassured him that we are born with innate guilt and that it is normal to have phantasies of attacks on mother's other babies and to fear reprisal. As I have discussed elsewhere (Adams, 2002), in interpreting dreams, Freud focussed on reconstructing from the past, looking for repressed memories, symbolism and 'day residue'. He did not have a clear understanding of unconscious phantasies. Freud seemed almost persecuted by the 'unruly' dream activity which he called a 'conglomerate' of unconscious fantasies. In his confusion, he tried to dismiss it as an illusion (Freud, 1900, p. 581). Today, Freud's technique of 'free association' is valued for illuminating the phantasies and what is emotionally alive in the patient's internal world.

When one of my replacement child patients began reading Melanie Klein and became aware of the extraordinary activity in the internal world—the projection, the splitting, the love and the hate, the death wishes—she could start separating herself from the murderers and dead babies in her nightmares. Jealousy towards siblings and hatred towards the mother suddenly became an everyday part of the child's inner world and not unique to her.

Rizzuto describes Freud's early experience:

He was born to parents who were mourning. The deaths of his paternal grandfather and of his maternal uncle and little brother, both named Julius, marked him for the rest of his life. In his childhood depression he found in his nurse a person who offered him the 'means for living and going on living'. She was abruptly taken away from him, never to be seen again. Then he clung to his father, admiring the powerful man. He too let him down. He experienced the move to Vienna and his father's incompetence in supporting the family as a catastrophe.

(2007, p. 40)

She adds that, for Freud, God could not offer protection or consolation against the terrors of childhood or the tragedies of adult life: 'The only choice for Freud, the mature man, the "godless Jew", was to become self-sufficient, renounce the wish for consolation, and stoically accept reality as it is' (Rizzuto, 2007, p. 40). Writing to his future bride, Freud said: 'I believe people see something alien in me and the real reason for this is that in my youth I was never young and now that I am entering the age of maturity [thirty] I cannot mature properly' (Freud, 1960, p. 202).

Where is the Mother?

In his biography of Freud, Joel Whitebook asks the question, 'Where is the mother?!' He says her absence is itself a 'presence':

> The mother is largely missing from Freud's self-analysis and from the *Interpretation of Dreams*, the work that grew out of it; from his *Case Histories*, where she cries out for inclusion; from his theories of development and pathogenesis; and from his patriarchal theories of culture and religion.
>
> (2017, p. 2)

James Joyce was also silent about his mother except in his fiction. In *Ulysses*, she appears in his nightmares as persecutor.

Freud's mother, Amalie, withdrew both physically and emotionally after the death of his brother. As Whitebook says, following Andre Green:

> The most disastrous depression is that which follows 'the death of a child at an early age'. With the death of Julius, in the context of numerous earlier losses, Amalie became 'a dead mother'.
>
> (2017, p. 37)

Whitebook believes there was a good attachment between Freud and his mother during his first year, but the brother's sudden death and the mother's disappearance left Freud feeling 'unlovable' and with a lifelong terror of helplessness along with the feelings of self-reproach. There was warmth and caring from his father, Jakob, and from his nursemaid (traumatically dismissed before he was three), but the sense of abandonment and betrayal by his mother (who then had five daughters and another son) stayed with him. Turning again to Whitebook:

> Green argues that the mother's psychological death—which, as a rule, occurs suddenly and unexpectedly—'brutally' transforms the

child's image of her from 'a living object' and 'a source of vitality . . . into a distant toneless [and] practically inanimate...figure'. In short, she becomes '*a mother who remains alive and physically present but who is, so to speak, psychically dead in the eyes of the young child in her care*'. The 'frozen' character of the maternal object prevents internalizations that are necessary for healthy development, and this creates significant lacunae in the individual's psychic structure. In an attempt to compensate for those 'gaps in the fabric of the self' and to grapple with the 'massive loss of meaning' that the catastrophe precipitates, individuals suffering from the dead mother syndrome often resort to extensive intellectualization and become involved in a compulsive search for meaning. Who fits this description better than Freud?

(*Ibid*, p. 38)

Amalie was described as narcissistic, volatile and self-centred: 'an emotionally exhausting, wilful mother, a mother who could see herself in her children but could not see them in their own right' (*Ibid*, p. 36). In her research, Rizzuto found that, in Freud, most quotations, dreams, memories and associations connect his mother to death and to God (1998, p. 226). He never said that he loved her, and when she died, he did not attend the funeral. Her death, as he wrote to Ferenczi, gave him 'a feeling of liberation, of release, which I think I also understand. I was not free to die as long as she was alive, and now I am' (Freud, 1960, p. 400).

Intrusive Identification

How does a child negotiate the aesthetic conflict if the nurturing mother, in her sudden grief, turns to stone and the music of her voice is silenced? In *The Apprehension of Beauty*, Donald Meltzer describes the extraordinary impact on the infant of the presence of the mother who has held him in her womb, brought him into the world, feeds him at her breast, talks/sings to him and responds to his gaze. Inter-uterine studies have made us aware of the impact in the womb of the mother's voice and mood—Meltzer talks of the music of her voice 'shifting from major to minor key' (1988, p. 22). Hindle cites neurophysiological research which indicates that the capacity to hear is fully developed by four months' gestation and that the mother's voice is not only heard by the unborn child, but 'its sound and timbre, its rhythmical and musical qualities become the actual base for its future linguistic code' (2000, p. 1194).

Both Freud and Joyce were devoted to language itself. Freud spent hours as an analyst listening intently to his patients' words. Yerushalmi says,

> Freud retained…a primal belief in the potency of words, whether as a vehicle for his conscious thoughts and teachings or as a means of access to the unconscious. For all the advances in his own understanding of what takes place in the psychoanalytic situation, he never lost faith that words lie at the very heart of it.
>
> (1992, pp. 1–20)

Joyce, always declaring his love of language, toiled over sentences, putting the words in the right order to make them sing. Harry Levin:

> His peculiar strength lay in speculation, introspection, and an almost hyper-aesthetic capacity for rendering sensations. These are poetic attributes, and his successes are the achievements of a poet—in arranging verbal harmonies which touch off emotional responses.
>
> (1960, p. 154)

Freud and Joyce also spent their lives getting into the minds of others and into their own writing. Anna Freud, on her father's 80th birthday, inscribed a book to him: '*Writing books as the supreme defence against all dangers from within and without*'.

Meltzer, in *The Claustrum* (1992), describes the intrusive identification adopted by the child who, in the presence now of a 'dead mother', feeling cut adrift and seeking safety, unconsciously enters inside the mother. This way the child becomes one with her. It also has the effect of eliminating her in his mind, so he can deny her separateness and never have to lose her. In Chapter 5, I discuss how this form of intrusive relating leaves one isolated and imprisoned.

Freud is described as fearful of the all-encompassing union between mother and child and focussed for protection on the father. His mother was also a constant source of anxiety for him as she herself remained anxious about any death. As described by Clark:

> According to a letter Freud wrote…in 1925, Amalie Freud could not tolerate hearing about any death in the family. Through a familial conspiracy of silence, she was protected from the knowledge of several deaths over many years: 'We made a secret of all the losses in the family'.
>
> (1980, p. 481)

Pre-Oedipal Guilt

For both Freud and Joyce, as well as the 'replacement child' patients I refer to in this book, a sense of guilt seemed ever present. This is a tragic, misplaced delusional guilt. In the mind of the child, negative wishes against their siblings are tantamount to having *caused* the deaths. James Joyce disparaged psychoanalysis for himself, worried, perhaps, about the guilt he felt, but he tried to analyse his own disturbing dreams. Like my patients, his nightmares contributed to his sense of being a murderer. His books are full of guilt and blame. In *Ulysses*, Stephen's guilt is linked to denying the wishes of his mother and the church, as well as sexual transgression. The themes in *Finnegans Wake* include virtually every one of the 'typical dreams' described by Freud (Norris, 1977, pp. 98–118). Following Freud, he tried to understand the guilt as Oedipal, but it never quite works. Joyce seems to be searching. Freud located guilt as Oedipal, father/son rivalry, but most powerful for him was presumably guilt towards his mother. In Sprengnether's view:

> Freud's difficulty acknowledging feelings of hostility toward the mother is not only an important element of his personal life, but also an important influence on the creation of the Oedipal theory: the Oedipal theory deflects rage toward the mother, redirecting it toward the father.
>
> (1995, p. 46)

Whitebook describes dissociation in Freud:

> 'The traumatic experiences of Freud's first four years were dissociated, not integrated into a coherent sense of self'. Although this defensive dissociation protected Freud and allowed him to function at an exceptionally high level, it also largely cut him off from the realm of early pre-Oedipal experience. And because the world of archaic experience was too dangerous for Freud to explore—to do so might bring back the overwhelming anxiety and sense of helplessness he had experienced as a child—it could not be integrated into his theory.
>
> (2017, pp. 50–51)

The 'Oceanic' & the Aesthetic Conflict

A notable difference between Freud and Joyce is the love of music so present in Joyce and so missing in Viennese Freud. Freud explained his difficulty appreciating music: 'Some rationalistic, or perhaps analytic, turn of mind in me rebels against being moved by a thing without knowing why I am thus affected and what it is that affects me' (1914, p. 210). He prevented a sister from learning the piano and the piano was removed from the apartment. One can sympathise as it was a big family in a small apartment, but Freud's objection was more profound. His strong aversion to music with its 'contentless forms and intensities and unaccountable emotions' was almost unheard of in Vienna. His mother was very musical and wanted her daughters to learn the piano. Whitebook quotes Breger who interprets Freud's almost phobic reaction as an angry rejection of this mother who had infuriated him with her desertion to depression, other pregnancies and all her other crimes:

> Because Freud viewed his volatile Galician mother as the exemplification of emotionality, his attempt to put 'a lid on her musical interest' represented 'part of his wider need to control emotion' in general.
>
> (2017, p. 55)

He came to enjoy opera later in life, helped by the libretto. But his fear of music is described by Whitebook as similar to his fear of the feminine, of emotion and the 'oceanic' (2017, p. 405).

Perhaps Joyce tried to manage the aesthetic conflict and losing his mother by intrusive identification, essentially entering and taking over the 'other'. About his wish to get inside, Joyce wrote to his wife, Nora:

> O that I could nestle in your womb like a child born of your flesh and blood, be fed by your blood, sleep in the warm secret gloom of your body. …My little mother, take me into the dark sanctuary of your womb.
>
> (Ellmann, 1975, p. 169)

In *Ulysses*, he enters inside and *becomes* Molly Bloom in her long soliloquy. There is no separation between narrator and character. It is as though, intruding into Molly and drawing her into his own fantasies, he starts to sense a pornographic quality and even has her say, 'Oh Jamesy let me up out of this pooh'. *Finnegans Wake* is different and non-intrusive. In the 'Anna Livia Plurabelle' section, for example, we are listening to the two washerwomen talking *about* Anna (not from within), gossiping and speculating. Edna O'Brien describes Anna as 'too rarefied and too remote':

> Whereas Molly Bloom was all flesh and appetite, Anna is all essence. We do not get inside her mind or know the registers of

her disenchantments as she passes from youth to age, except for a rare and piercing lamentation—'Is there one who understands me?'.

(2017)

The 'Anna Livia' section is bawdy and risque, but not pornographic. Its lyrical passages are the poetry of a son who has internalised the music of his mother's voice:

> anna loavely long pair of inky Italian moostarshes
> glistering with boric vaseline and frangipani.
> Puh!
> How unwhisperably so!
>   (FW 182)

Internalising the mother is different from entering her and intruding into her. It takes in a sense of her while allowing her separateness and unknowability.

Joyce spoke openly of his father's beautiful tenor voice, but he was silent about the music he shared with his mother. She died of liver cancer when he was only 21, and he spent her last few months playing the piano and singing for her. He then fled into exile and devoted himself to bringing alive the mother he'd lost and the Dublin he loved, preserving them in *Ulysses* and *Finnegans Wake*.

As I describe in Chapter 3, Joyce could rail at his dead mother and express his grief when she appeared in his nightmares in *Ulysses*. This seemed to free him. But Freud, whose mother did not die until he was 74, repressed his rage and remained the dutiful son.

Rivals & Revenants

In his *Introductory Lectures*, Freud observes,

> A small child does not necessarily love his brothers and sisters; often he obviously does not. There is no doubt that he hates them as his competitors, and it is a familiar fact that this attitude often persists for long years, till maturity is reached or even later, without interruption. This hostile attitude can be observed most easily ... when a new baby brother or sister appears. It usually meets with a very unfriendly reception...every opportunity is taken of disparaging the new arrival and attempts to injure him and even murderous assaults are not unknown.
>
> (1916, pp. 204–205)

Freud was aware of his intense rivalry with younger colleagues, such as Breuer, Fliess and Jung. It was revealed in his dreams, such as the 'Non Vixit' and 'Irma Injection' dreams. As well as the themes of the dead child and the dead mother which appear frequently in *The Interpretation of Dreams*, the idea of revenants, the return of the dead brother, also occurs. Freud linked his three separate fainting attacks when visiting Jung to the rivalry he felt and to the death of his brother.

In a letter to Jung, he exclaimed, 'Why in God's name did I allow myself to follow you into this field?' James Fisher (2008) looks at the intensity and Lear-like, father/son rivalry between Freud and Jung, but Jung is also the brother-usurper. In the 'Non Vixit' dream, Freud says to the brother: 'It serves you right if you had to make way for me. Why did you try to push *me* out of the way? I don't need you' (1900, p. 331). Clark points out that:

> The delight which Freud felt in the dream at being able to control the *revenants* and make them disappear appears to indicate his anxiety that these figures might indeed come back and punish him for his aggressive thoughts.
>
> (1980, p. 316)

Part of the role of the mother is to help the child distinguish between fears and reality but left on his own, in the presence of a 'dead mother', the child seeks control. Both Freud and Joyce devoted their lives to creating great literary structures to give them security and control.

'Anna O'—Martha Pappenheim

A significant figure in Freud's life was Martha Pappenheim, a patient of Breuer's and a 'replacement child'. Freud's *Studies on Hysteria* (1895) was co-written with Breuer and based on his description of her treatment. While aware of the fact that Pappenheim ('Anna O') had lost two sisters in childhood, Freud and Breuer (also a replacement child) focussed on Oedipal issues, diagnosing hysteria, seemingly neglecting the impact of her earliest trauma. It is disturbing to think that Freud based key aspects of psychoanalysis on this case. Pappenheim became progressively worse, suffering from frightening hallucinations. When her mind was clear, she would complain of 'the profound darkness in her head, of not being able to think, of becoming blind and deaf, of having two selves, a real one and an evil one which forced her to behave badly'. Pollock describes how, in an orthodox household like Pappenheim's, the death of children would have been remembered:

> The death anniversaries of the two sisters were probably observed regularly. ...We know that children who are dead may remain powerfully in the mother's mind and so can become even more important rivals for the surviving sibling. ...The dead sibling usually remains remembered at the age he was at the time of his death, and hence there is some arrest of the image of the sibling in the minds of the survivors.
>
> (1972, p. 478)

Joan Riviere

The psychoanalyst, Joan Riviere was born, like Joyce, one year after the death of her parents' firstborn son. She was in analysis first with Ernest Jones and then, when that broke down, with Freud. Neither Jones nor Freud focussed on the sibling death and Freud felt he failed with her. He wrote to Jones:

> [Riviere] cannot tolerate praise, triumph or success, not any better than failure, blame and repudiation. She gets unhappy in both cases.... So she has arranged for herself what we call 'eine Zwickmühle' [a dilemma]. ...Whenever she has got a recognition, a favour or a present, she is sure to become unpleasant and aggressive and to lose respect for the analyst. You know what that means, it is an infallible sign of a deep sense of guilt.
>
> (Hughes, 2004, p. 85)

Freud saw it as a conflict between Ego and Ideal, but in Chapter 5, I discuss fear of success as linked to the survivor guilt in my replacement child patients. Riviere herself, in late life, wrote a detailed paper on Ibsen whose parents lost their firstborn son. In writing about *The Master Builder*, she asks 'where is the mother', the same question that was asked about Shakespeare, Freud and Joyce:

> The mother-figure of the Builder's inner world is... almost conspicuous by her absence. True, she it is whom he is for ever creating and recreating anew in his churches and homes; but that relation is far from the simple direct one to a mother. ...There is no woman in the play who is actually a mother.
>
> (Riviere, 1952, p. 178)

Riviere talks about the dead babies, Solness' feelings of guilt and the way wishes, if they become reality, continue to persecute. The play turns on whether Solness was to blame for the mother's babies' deaths or not (*Ibid*, pp. 174–175).

Harry Guntrip

Another example of failure to recognise the impact of losing a sibling is described by the psychoanalyst, Harry Guntrip. He had analyses with Fairburn and Winnicott and felt let down by both:

> I went to [Fairburn] to break through the amnesia for that trauma of my brother's death. There, I felt, lay the cause of my vague background experiences of schizoid isolation and unreality. After brother Percy's death I entered on four years of active battle with mother to force her 'to relate', and then gave it up and grew away from her. [Fairburn] repeatedly brought me back to oedipal three-person libidinal and anti-libidinal conflicts in my 'inner world'. ...I began to insist that my real problem was ...mother's basic 'failure to relate at all' right from the start. ...I felt oedipal analysis kept me marking time on the same spot.
>
> (1996, p. 743)

Rainer Maria Rilke

Neither Freud nor Joyce had a mother who tried to make them the child who had died in the way that the poet Rilke's mother did. Some parents gave their child the same name as the child who had died, Van Gogh, Beethoven, Stendhal and Dali, for example. But Rilke was called by his dead sister's name, Rene Maria, and at times dressed in girl's clothes.

> His mother had wanted a girl, and christened her son and only child René Maria. 'I had to wear very beautiful clothes and went about until school years like a little girl; I believe my mother played with me as with a big doll'. 'I see her only occasionally, but...every encounter is a sort of relapse'.
>
> (Banville, 2013)

His was a more disturbing and confusing experience with his mother: 'From her to me no warm breeze ever blew' (Rilke, 1981, p. 65). Ron Britton describes the way Rilke wrote to fill an emptiness inside: 'the inner void begins to transform into a container for thought, and by naming his losses he moves from paranoid-schizoid to depressive mode' (Edwards, 2005, p. 323). But Rilke was never able to achieve the inner contentment that Joyce found.

The Philippson Bible—Freud's 'Book of Kells'

In Chapter 10, I describe Joyce's lifelong fascination with the Irish *Book of Kells*, the elaborately illuminated Latin copy of the Four Gospels. As well as portraits of the four evangelists and scenes from the Biblical text, it has Celtic motifs, imaginary creatures and plants swirling around words and images. The *Book of Kells* has similarities with the 1858 *Philippson Bible* that Freud grew up with. Unlike most Bibles, it was heavily illustrated with wood engravings depicting scenes beyond the mere Biblical. As Whitebook describes:

> It contained 685 illustrations meant to evoke the historical, cultural, and physical context of the biblical story. They depicted landscapes, towns, plants, animals, coins, utilitarian objects from everyday life, and even Egyptian gods—that is to say, images of foreign deities. As Jacob Freud surely knew, all these elements of the volume he chose to purchase—the German translation, the scientific commentaries, and especially the illustrations, which violate 'God's stern prohibition on using images' (Gresser 1994, 41)—would have been viewed as sacrilegious from the vantage point of the Orthodox world in which he had been brought up.
>
> (2017, p. 22)

In his autobiography, Freud wrote: 'My deep engrossment in the Bible story (almost as soon as I learned the art of reading) had, as I recognized much later, an enduring effect upon the direction of my interest' (1925, p. 8). Both Freud and Joyce turned away from the religion of their parents and this contributed to the guilt they felt. However, their final works, *Moses and Monotheism* and *Finnegans Wake*, both published in 1939, represent a 'homecoming'—for Freud to Judaism, and for Joyce to family—and reflect the learning they absorbed from their 'deep engrossment' in these Biblical tomes.

Moses & Monotheism—A Return to the Father

In my final chapter, I describe *Finnegans Wake* as Joyce's 'return to the father'. This could also be a description of *Moses and Monotheism*.

Both fathers were a vital figure in their son's life. Describing *Moses and Monotheism*, Ostow writes:

> We have here a return of his own repressed love for his father. His father encouraged his study of classical Jewish literature and Jewish history. In his adolescence, during the liberal period of Austrian history, he changed his name, discarded the Philippson Bible, spoke disparagingly of the Jewish religion and its observances, and of East European Jews who were crowding in Vienna, and he aspired to identification with German culture. But the resurgence of anti-Semitism following 1880, forced him into assertiveness about being Jewish, and in fact to militancy. …Finally, we see Freud at the end of his life, completely immersed in the Bible story, in subsequent Jewish history, in Zionism, and in movements promoting Jewish culture.
>
> (1989, p. 490)

Jonte-Pace (2001) sees the book as Freud's emotional and intellectual homecoming to Judaism, to the 'witty, enlightened faith' of his father Jakob and sees Freud as a kind of a heroic composite of Joseph and Moses.

Joyce through *Finnegans Wake* reunites with the mother. Freud sought comfort, it seems, from the myriad antiquities that he began collecting after his father's death. Among the collection that he took with him from Vienna were 600 Egyptian items, including numerous mother/child pairs. Ana-Marie Rizzuto writes:

> He had all his antiquities with him, all his gods that he talked to, and his personal, intellectual life there with him. Freud's unmet need for protection and consolation prompted him to reject the God of his father. Yet his actual father could offer him a loving and playful presence, which he needed and cherished. In an unconscious and roundabout way, Freud had created his ad hoc ancestor temple and cult. He even opted to die not in his bedroom but in his office, where the antiquities were.
>
> (2007, p. 41)

In the next chapter, I look at people's impressions of Joyce, many commenting on the combination of brilliance and fragility. One could say the same about Freud. It seems remarkable how much this Vienna Jew and Dublin Catholic have in common, how hard they worked at their self-analysis, how revolutionary their thinking—and how engaged with them we remain.

References

Adams, M. (2002). Dreams and the Discovery of the Internal World, *The Journal of the British Association of Psychotherapists*, 40: 1.

Banville, J. (2013). Study the Panther. Rilke's 'Letters to a Young Poet', *New York Review of Books*, January.

Breuer, J., & Freud, S. (1893–1895). *Studies in Hysteria*, SE 2.

Britton, R. (1998). *Belief and Imagination: Explorations in Psychoanalysis*. London: Routledge.

Clark, R. W. (1980). *Freud, The Man and the Cause: A Biography*. New York: Random House.

Edwards, J. (2005). Before the Threshold: Destruction, Reparation and Creativity in Relation to the Depressive Position, *Journal of Child Psychotherapy*, 31(3): 317–333.

Ellmann, R., ed. (1992). *Selected Letters of James Joyce*. London: Faber and Faber.

Fisher, J. V. (2008). Abdication of a Father: Some Reflections on the Freud-Jung Correspondence1, *British Journal of Psychotherapy*, 24: 273–298.

Freud, S. (1900). *The Interpretation of Dreams,* SE 4: ix, 627.Freud, S. (1914). *The Moses of Michelangelo*, SE 14: 211.

Freud, S. (1916). *Introductory Lectures on Psycho-Analysis*. SE 15:1–240

Freud, S. (1925). *An Autobiographical Study,* SE 20.

Freud, S. (1931). *Female Sexuality*, SE 21: 221–244.

Freud, S. (1939). *Moses and Monotheism: Three Essays*. Standard Edition 23: 1–137.

Freud, E. ed. (1960). *Letters of Sigmund Freud*. New York: Basic Books.

Guntrip, H. (1996). My Experience of Analysis with Fairbairn and Winnicott, *The International Journal of Psychoanalysis*, 77: 739–754.

Hamilton, J. W. (1976). Some Comments about Freud's Conceptualization of the Death Instinct, *International Review of Psycho-Analysis*, 3: 151–164.

Harrison, I. (1979). On Freud's View of the Infant-Mother Relationship and of the Oceanic Feeling—Some Subjective Influences, *Journal of the American Psychoanalytic Association*, 27: 399–342.

Hindle, D. (2000). L'Enfant Et Les Sortilèges Revisited, *International Journal of Psychoanalysis*, 81(6): 1185–1119.

Hughes, J. M. (2004). *From Obstacle to Ally: The Evolution of Psychoanalytic Practice*. Routledge.

Jonte-Pace, D. (2001). *Speaking the Unspeakable. Religion, Misogyny, and the Uncanny Mother in Freud's Cultural Texts*. Berkeley: University of California Press.

Joyce, J. (2012). *Finnegans Wake*. Oxford: Oxford World Classics.

McGuire, W. (ed.) (1974) *The Freud—Jung Letters: The Correspondence between Sigmund Freud and C.G. Jung*. Princeton, NJ: Princeton University Press.

Meltzer, D. (1988). *The Apprehension of Beauty: The Role of Aesthetic Conflict in Development, Art and Violence*. London: Karnac Books.

Meltzer, D. (1992). *The Claustrum: An Investigation of Claustrophobic Phenomena*. Strath Tay: Clunie Press.

Norris, M. (1977). *The Decentered Universe of Finnegans Wake: A Structural Analysis.* New York: The Johns Hopkins University Press.

O'Brien, E. (2017). *Foreword* to *Anna Livia Plurabelle.* London: Faber & Faber.

Ostow, M. (1989). Sigmund and Jakob Freud and the Philippson Bible—*(With an Analysis of the Birthday Inscription), International Review of Psychoanalysis,* 16: 483–492.

Pollock, G. H. (1968). The Possible Significance of Childhood Object Loss in the Josef Breuer-Bertha Pappenheim (Anna O.)-Sigmund Freud Relationship, *Journal of the American Psychoanalytic Association,* 16: 711–739.

Pollock, G. H. (1972). Bertha Pappenheim's Pathological Mourning: Possible Effects of Childhood Sibling Loss, *Journal of the American Psychoanalytic Association,* 20: 476–493.

Rilke, R. M. (1981). *An Unofficial Rilke,* ed. and trans. M Hamburger. London: Anvil Poetry.

Riviere, J. (1952). The Inner World in Ibsen's Master-Builder, *International Journal of Psycho-Analysis,* 33: 173–180.

Rizzuto, A. (1998). *Why Did Freud Reject God? A Psychodynamic Interpretation.* New Haven, CT: Yale University Press.

Rizzuto, A. (2007). God in the Mind: The Psychodynamics of an Unusual Relationship, *Annual of Psychoanalysis,* 35: 25–46.

Schur, M. (1969). The Background of Freud's "Disturbance" on the Acropolis, *American Imago,* 26: 303–323.

Schur, M. (1972). *Freud: Living and Dying.* New York: International UP.

Sprengnether, M. (1995). Reading Freud's Life, *American Imago,* 52(1): 9–54.

Whitebook, J. (2017). *Freud. An Intellectual Biography.* Cambridge: Cambridge University Press.

Yerushalmi, Y. H. (1992). The Moses of Freud and the Moses of Schoenberg— On Words, Idolatry, and Psychoanalysis, *Psychoanalytic Study of the Child,* 47: 1–20.

2 Images of Joyce

'This bizarre and wonderful creature'

In James Joyce's first school photograph, at Clongowes College, he sits cross legged, alone in the front (https://www.clongowes. net/2022/02/07). He is very small, the youngest boy in the school. Asked his age upon arrival at the school he said 'half past six'. This became his nickname, the other boys perhaps not wanting to take in how very young he was. He slept in the infirmary so that a nurse could look after him. He was desperately homesick and unhappy. Issues of banishment haunted him all his life and one can see why. For Joyce it becomes self-banishment and self-exile, 'exiled in on himself', as he put it. He later identified in this way with Shakespeare, another replacement child. In *Ulysses* he writes about Shakespeare:

> The note of banishment, banishment from the heart, banishment from the home, sounds uninterruptedly from The Two Gentlemen of Verona onward till Prospero breaks his staff, buries it certain fathoms in the earth and drowns his book.
>
> (Kiberd, lxxii)

Being exceptionally bright and with a precocious belief in himself, Joyce quickly developed ways of surviving, and of excelling—techniques that would serve him all his life. During his three years at the Jesuit, Clongowes Wood College, he became head of his class. Drawing on his retentive memory, he could quickly commit both prose and verse to memory and even keep whole visual scenes in his head undiminished. He was also a good athlete and did well in cricket in spite of being younger and smaller than the other boys. For all his later repudiation of religion, he felt the majesty of Church, embraced religious instruction and was chosen as altar boy. All his life he attracted attention and already at his first school he was described as 'the most vivid boy in the line' (*JJ*, pp. 29–31).

DOI: 10.4324/9781003309925-3

It is fascinating to read people's reminiscences of him. He may have been demanding, especially of his brother Stanislas, but he was many things and obviously elicited great love. Robert Reid said, 'Joyce's gentleness, sensitivity and loneliness of spirit made a deep impression on me' (1990, p. 112). Nancy Cunard called him 'a tall cathedral-spire of a man' (*Ibid*, p. 128). His great friend, Eugene Jolas, wrote: 'When he was in the mood, his talk, given his mellifluous Dublin speech, was a ripple of illuminating ideas and words' (*Ibid*, xv). Waiters loved Joyce. He gave millionaire tips and, better, he always asked the waiter's advice...whether they preferred Racine to Corneille or the other way about (Stephens, 1990, p. 111).

There are two volumes of recollections of Joyce by his close friends. Despite his shyness and retreat into writing, he maintained close friendships throughout his life, mostly male, some Irish, such as Samuel Beckett and Padraic Colum, but mainly Europeans that he knew in Trieste and Paris. Their descriptions of Joyce are a beauty in themselves. Joyce leaned heavily on friends to help him, especially given his poor eyesight, but he wasn't resented for it. His main focus in life was always his writing. He loved spending time with those who were genuinely interested in his work and after years of struggle getting published, he relished the support he was getting later in life.

His male friendships have a 'lost brother' feel to them. I describe his friendship with Oliver St John Gogarty ('Buck Mulligan' in *Ulysses*) in Chapter 8. Another deep friendship was with Samuel Beckett. When Beckett was in hospital in Paris after being mugged in the street, Joyce visited him with Nino Frank who wrote:

> I have never felt so close to Ireland, to its sentimental isolation, to the very air of *Ulysses*, as I did that day, sitting between those two brothers, in their shape and their keenness like twin knife blades. The elder and the younger were united by a profound bond.
>
> (1979, p. 96)

As a young man, Joyce was considered arrogant and unapproachable but in exile he changed and is described as a gentle, fun-loving family man. It is hard to think of other writers, except perhaps Samuel Beckett and Seamus Heaney, who have elicited such tender recollections. Those who knew him were bewitched by special qualities and an aura about him. The Surrealist writer Philippe Soupault who knew him in Paris, described him as 'the most affectionate, the most sensitive of friends, and the one who had the greatest impact on me'. He called Joyce 'a great poet, who knew what poetry meant and who lived by it and for it' (1979, pp. 108–109).

Another friend in Paris, the French literary critic, Louis Gillet, wrote in 1931:

> This terrible nay-sayer was a family man; …his family was for him a sheet-anchor, the sacred Ark. He was attached to rites, dates, anniversaries, to a secret calendar to which he ascribed a superstitious importance.
>
> (1979, p. 181)

The Irish poet, Padraic Colum, a lifelong friend and fellow exile, described Joyce as a student:

> He was very noticeable amongst the crowd of students who frequented the National Library or who sauntered along the streets between Nelson's Pillar and Stephens' [*sic*] Green. He was tall and slender when I knew him first, with a Dantesque face and steely blue eyes. The costume I see him in as I look back includes a peaked cap and tennis shoes more or less white. He used to swing along the street carrying in his hand an ash-plant by way of a cane. Stories were told about his arrogance.
>
> (1990, p. 37)

Harold Nicolson, in his diary, described visiting Joyce in Paris:

> The sitting room was like a small salon at a provincial hotel, and the unreal effect was increased by there being florists' baskets about with arranged flowers. Joyce glided in. It was evident that he had just been shaving. He was very spruce and nervous and natty. Great rings upon little twitching fingers. Huge concave glasses which flicked reflections of lights as he moved his head like a bird, turning with that definite insistence to the speaker as blind people do who turn to the sound of the voice. …He was very courteous as shy people are. His beautiful voice trilled on slowly like Anna Livia Plurabelle. He has the most lovely voice I know—liquid and soft with undercurrents of gurgle.
>
> (2004, p. 125)

Mario Nordio, an Italian friend of 60 years said:

> Everyone was struck at once by his blue eyes. Although he was near sighted, his eyes were very sharp and keen, flashing with a deep, intelligent light under his spectacles. His hand was cold and

inert, and he never shook hands properly. As he walked the streets, his legs looked like a pair of rigid compasses. ... His mind was nimble and open to every problem of that time and to broad questions of any sort. His conversation was always vivid, incisive, and so varied that nobody could foresee its subjects. It was often full of humour and ironic hidden thoughts. As he passed from one subject to another, he would season his speech with anecdotes in his favourite form of apologues.

(1990, p. 57)

It is hard to put these fond and gentle images of Joyce together with the physical and emotional struggle he endured. He described his youth as 'exceptionally violent and painful' but his adult life was difficult too. For most of it, he had little money. He had numerous operations on his eyes but remained half-blind. The constant in his life was Nora. She and Joyce remained devoted to each other and Joyce's friends seemed as charmed by her as they were by Joyce: 'Cheerfulness predominated. ... There I saw Mrs Joyce, a beauty faithful to her portrait, barely powdered by the years, patient, gentle, and infinitely distant' (Frank, 1979, p. 89). Louis Menand writes:

Joyce had known only prostitutes and proper middle-class girls. Nora was something new, an ordinary woman who treated him as an ordinary man. The moral simplicity of what happened between them seems to have stunned him. It was elemental, a gratuitous act of loving that had not involved flattery or deceit, and that was unaccompanied by shame or guilt. That simplicity became the basis of their relationship.

(2012)

Towards the end of his life Nino Frank described a new solitude in Joyce, as his intimate circle was mainly Samuel Beckett, Eugene Jolas, Paul Leon. His work on *Finnegans Wake* was 'an incessant labour but left him a few moments nearly every day for an often somewhat demonic gaiety'. Having earlier described Joyce as a kind of Don Quixote, this was Frank's final view of him: 'He left me brandishing his white cane, and I seemed to behold the weightless walk of Oedipus' (1979, pp. 91–93).

After Joyce's death, Samuel Beckett wrote:

Our dealings were entirely those of friends...He showed me the greatest kindness and generosity. I saw him for the last time in

Vichy in 1940. I still think of him as one of the greatest literary geniuses of all time...He gave me an insight into what the words 'to be an artist' mean. I think of him with unqualified admiration, affection and gratitude.

(2020, pp. 463–464)

References

Beckett, S. (2020). *The Letters of Samuel Beckett 1941–1956*, in G. Craig, M. Dow Fehsenfeld, D Gunn and L. Overbeck, eds. Cambridge: Cambridge UP.

Colum, P. (1990). James Joyce as a Young Man, in E. H. Mikhail, ed. *James Joyce: Interviews & Recollections*. Macmillan Press. p. 37–40.

Cunard, N. (1990). 'Visits from James Joyce', in E. H. Mikhail, ed., *James Joyce: Interviews & Recollections*. Macmillan Press, pp. 127–129.

Ellmann, R. (1982). *James Joyce*, first revised edition of the 1959 classic. Oxford: Oxford University Press.

Frank, N. (1979). 'The Shadow That Had Lost Its Man', in W. Potts, ed., *Portraits of the Artist in Exile. Recollections of James Joyce by Europeans*. Seattle: University of Washington Press, p. 74.

Gillet, L. (1979). 'Farewell to Joyce', in W. Potts, ed., *Portraits of the Artist in Exile. Recollections of James Joyce by Europeans*. Seattle: University of Washington Press, pp. 165–169.

Kiberd, D. (1992). Introduction: James Joyce, *Ulysses, Annotated Student Edition*. Penguin, pp. ix–lxxx.

Menand, L. (2012). Silence, Exile, Punning. James Joyce's Chance Encounters, *New Yorker*, July.

Nicolson, N. ed. (2004). *The Harold Nicolson Diaries 1907–1964*. London: Orion Books.

Nordio, M. (1990). 'My First English Teacher', in E. H. Mikhail, ed., *James Joyce: Interviews & Recollections*. Macmillan Press, p. 57.

Reid, R. (1990). 'I Meet, in Time and Space, James Joyce', in E. H. Mikhail, ed., *James Joyce: Interviews & Recollections*. Macmillan Press, pp. 111–114.

Soupault, P. (1990). 'Homage to James Joyce', in E. H. Mikhail, ed., *James Joyce: Interviews and Recollections*, pp. 113–141.

Stephens, J. (1990). 'The James Joyce I Knew', in E. H. Mikhail, ed., *James Joyce: Interviews and Recollections,* London: Macmillan Press, p. 111.

3 The 'Dead Mother'

'Dark Lady', 'ghoul, chewer of corpses!'

While it is breath-taking to see the intensity of feeling levelled at his dead mother by Stephen at the beginning of *Ulysses*, calling her 'ghoul, chewer of corpses', Joyce is surprisingly restrained in his allusions to her endless pregnancies—fifteen in all, five of whom died. There is a whole chapter, *Oxen of the Sun*, about Mrs Purefoy giving birth to yet another child (her 9th living child, 12th overall), but seen through Bloom's eyes it is a sympathetic portrait, with the callousness located in the rowdy medical students. In *Lestrygonians*, we have:

> Mina Purefoy swollen belly on a bed groaning to have a child tugged out of her. One born every second somewhere. Other dying every second. Since I fed the birds five minutes. Three hundred kicked the bucket. Other three hundred born, washing the blood off, all are washed in the blood of the lamb, bawling maaaaaa.
>
> (U, p. 208)

In *Finnegans Wake*, there is reference to Anna Livia delivering presents to her '111 children', but it is as though constant pregnancies were too painful an issue for Joyce to parody.

Joyce's mother had great love for him, but his experience would have been that she was always having new babies or grieving for lost ones. She was also deeply religious. In a letter he 'cursed the system which made her a victim—we were 17 in the family. I left the Catholic Church hating it most fervently'. In 1903, when only 21, Joyce was with her for the last few months of her life, playing the piano, singing and reading to her. Soon afterwards he wrote his highly praised last short story in *The Dubliners*, 'The Dead', a study in grief with some of Joyce's most beautiful writing. However, as Linda Paige describes, the reader of *Dubliners* soon discovers that there is something wrong with mother—all mothers:

DOI: 10.4324/9781003309925-4

The ambiguous mothers in *Dubliners* emerge paradoxical and enigmatic. Their 'goodness' most decidedly tainted, *Dubliners'* mothers often seem ineffectual or hardened, sometimes even wildly or sadly perverted. Their positive feelings for their children become suspect when tempered by their harshness or selfishness. Usually paralyzed, either physically, socially, or spiritually, the offspring of *Dubliners'* mothers suffer.

(1995, p. 119)

In her novel, *The Gathering*, Anne Enright writes about the mother's endless children:

My mother had twelve children and…seven miscarriages. The holes in her head are not her fault. Even so, I have never forgiven her any of it. I just can't. …I do not forgive her the whole tedious litany of Midge, Bea, Ernest…. I don't forgive her those dead children either.

(2007, p. 7)

My focus is on how much Joyce could have been affected by the 'dead mother' syndrome in infancy, given his mother's grief at having lost her first child, already pregnant again with her third and her husband devastated. Andre Green identifies the death of a child at an early age as 'the most serious instance' of the 'dead mother': 'The mother remains physically present, but she has psychically "died" for the surviving child' (1986, p. 149). It is curious that the concept of the 'dead mother' is now well recognised but less often linked with the fate of the replacement child for whom the pain of the loss of the mother in this way is an overriding feature.

How much can we locate the origin of Joyce's lifelong emotional fragility to this early experience, notwithstanding his mother's obvious devotion to him? Was there an emptiness in him? In *Ulysses*, he writes about her death:

She was no more: the trembling skeleton of a twig burnt in the fire, an odour of rosewood and wetted ashes. She had saved him from being trampled underfoot and had gone, scarcely having been.

(U, 1922, 33)

The quality of anxiety and at times sheer terror experienced by Joyce sounded similar to my patients and was of the most primitive kind— that of the infant cut adrift. For my patients, anxiety attacks constantly threatened to engulf them.

In a harrowing tale of having been born six months after his brother's death, the playwright, David Storey, writes of his terror each morning, as if his brother's death were revivified each night:

> I had been plagued by attacks of terror from the age of three or four. By the time I was fifty-one, however, these sensations were with me all the while—all-consuming, all pervading, distorting everything I thought and felt.
>
> Our mother was three months gone the night you died. Half a lifetime later, I took to reading all I could on symptoms like mine—waking, as I did each morning, with the unmistakable impression that someone had died; the sensation that life, in the most frightening way possible, was coming to an end.
>
> (2021, pp. 3–4)

People close to Joyce knew of his fragility, both physical and emotional. He was described as living much of his life 'in desperate and tragic suffering' and 'living on the tightrope of his nerves' (Frank, 1979, p. 98). Arthur Power speaks of 'a melancholy that was always with him':

> A sensitive and poetic idealist, at war—a tentative, but never a conclusive, war—against the dark forces of primitive nature. And as life went on he became more and more interested intellectually in the workings of these forces. But it was his intellect which took him on, not his nature; for the man himself remained detached from life. Indeed, I think he was the most detached man I ever knew - detached in his work and detached in his pleasure.
>
> (1990, p. 173)

Margaret Anderson wrote:

> I had been prepared to see a sensitive man but … he gave me the impression of having less escape from suffering about irremediable things than anyone I had ever known…an impression borne out by nothing that he said so much as by the turn of his head, the droop of his wrist, the quiet tension of his face.
>
> (1990, p. 133)

Joyce's external life seemed one of constant battle, but his struggle with the debilitating nature of his own imagination and the fears it produced brought him close to madness. His phobias blighted his existence— seeing a rat would make him faint. In *Portrait*, he has Stephen say: 'I fear many things: dogs, horses, firearms, the sea, thunderstorms, machinery, country roads at night' (*P*, p. 264). He saw a malevolent reality behind them. He was highly superstitious. In Chapter 6, I link this with a proleptic imagination in the sense that superstition gives one a false kind of security, a 'knowing what will happen'. Richard Ellmann wrote: 'Joyce knew the superstitions of most of Europe, and adopted them all' (*JJ*, p. 517). In *Portrait,* Cranley comments on Stephen's fear of holy communion, fearing the host may be the body and blood of the son of God.

To lose a sibling and the mother's attention at this early stage of development, when there is a delicate back and forth between the use of fantasy and a gradual accommodating of reality, would be traumatic. Samuel Gerson eloquently expands the concept of the 'dead mother'. He describes the child in this situation as having lost the 'containing third' (Britton, 1989) and finding himself in the presence of a 'dead third':

> Rather than the potential for growth and security found in the notion of triangular space, the absence of an involved and caring other leaves only a dense and collapsed heap of destroyed internal and external objects for whom no one mourns. Imagine life, when the third is dead, when the container cracks and there is no presence ... to represent continuity. It is a world constituted by absence, where meaning is ephemeral and cynicism passes for wisdom.
>
> (2009, p. 1343)

In Ulysses, Stephen says: 'But thou has suckled me with a bitter milk; my moon and my sun thou has quenched forever. And thou has left me alone forever in the dark ways of my bitterness; and with a kiss of ashes hast thou kissed my mouth' (U, 387).

It is a core of emptiness, indeed, a hole, that Green describes: 'Identification with the dead mother, leaves a core that is frozen and therefore not really free to love another' (1986, pp. 153–154). The infant is suddenly faced with a mother 'absorbed by a bereavement which the infant had no way of understanding' (*Ibid*, p. 148). The result, he says, is 'the constitution of a hole in the texture of object-relations with the mother'. The mother continues to take care of the child, but 'her heart is not in it' (*Ibid*, p. 150). He describes the devastating consequence of this for the infant in that nothing makes sense and nothing seems to mean anything anymore.

Adiv-Ginach writes:

> The hole in the child's psychic world might be covered by a 'patched breast' and thus, in an ironic twist, artistic creativity and productive intellectualism are possible consequences of the dead

mother complex. Unfortunately, this process of sublimation is not altogether effective, as the subject will remain vulnerable on a particular point, which is his love life.

(2006, p. 51)

My patients spoke of an inner emptiness. They seemed almost to have *become* the missing heart of the mother, feeling, as they did, lost and 'floating' on the outside. One patient had a dream in which *her mother was running towards her, smiling and holding out her arms as if to hug her. But what her mother did not see was that there was a hole through the middle of her. The hole was large and cone shaped with metal sides. 'It was like looking through the barrel of a gun, or as though some surgical instrument had been inserted through her'.*

As she thought about the dream, she became more and more disturbed by the feeling of there being 'nothing inside', that 'something inside was missing'. She was shocked, feeling the figure in the dream was both herself and her mother. 'How could she not realise the hole was there?' she wondered. It was as though she had been 'shot through' by the realisation of how blind she has been to things missing. Not only were meaning and intimacy missing, it seemed *she* was actually missing. She herself belonged in this hole in the mother.

The patients' mothers were seen as wooden following the sibling's death. One patient's mother told her, 'my face cracked when the baby died', and her family literally took to their beds. The other patient learned the cello, practising for hours trying to bring life and music out of this wooden mother. They felt cut adrift.

Marguerite Reid writes about her work with a six-year-old boy, born following the cot death of his baby brother. She draws attention to the terror he experienced in relation to dead babies and dead objects as well as anxiety about his own death. She describes the existence of a destructive narcissistic structure that defended him against his feelings of terror that could not be contained by his grieving mother (1992).

Helene Deutsch, in a discussion of mothers mourning their deceased children, observes that the replacement child 'has very poor chances of conquering the mother's heart', and that 'during the period of mourning even the woman's own children are deprived of love and exposed to the painful silent reproach, "Why did you not die instead of the other?"' (Silver, 1983, p. 520). The picture my patients conveyed was of a mother turned away.

The depth of anger at the mother was expressed in the transference in the fear that I would be emotionally dead to them. Wanting to keep me alive, one patient was Joycean in her brilliance and entertainment.

She was also always on the alert for usurpers—to her, my other patients became threatening 'ghosts'—and expecting abandonment. Like Joyce, she was exceptionally well read, with a memory for everything. She avidly devoured extraordinary amounts of knowledge and information. Within the first few months of her analysis, she had not only noted the books on my shelves but ordered and read the complete works of Melanie Klein, quoting to me from the couch. In a poem to me she wrote, '*Star pupil, I out-Kleined them all, memorised each inch of your left wall, your blooded curtains*'. (My deep red curtains she linked with her mother's miscarriages.) She was so all-knowing and had such verbal facility and wit that in the analysis I had to withstand feeling both seduced and intimidated.

Thirst for Knowledge

Joyce dazzles with his encyclopaedic knowledge and verbal pyrotechnics and is described as a latter-day 'worldwide web', with a 'spider's eye' constantly absorbing information. From early in life he made copious and exhaustive lists and elaborate designs, eliciting from his father the wisecrack: 'if that fellow was dropped in the middle of the Sahara, he'd sit, be God, and make a map of it' (Kiberd, 1992, p. xxii). In *Ulysses* and *Finnegans Wake*, he includes the names of Shakespeare plays, all the books of the Bible, the chapters of the Koran, the rivers of the world, figures of rhetoric. Joyce mocks himself in *Finnegans Wake*:

> an you could peep inside the cerebralized saucepan of this eer ill-winded goodfornobody, you would see in his house of thoughtsam (was you, that is, decontamainated enough to look discarnate) what jetsam litterage of convolvuli of times lost or strayed, of lands derelict and of tongues laggin to.
>
> (FW 292)

Meltzer explains the thirst for knowledge and omniscience as the child being too impatient to learn from experience (1967, p. 142). For my patients, the intensity of feelings from their early experience felt barely survivable. They did not have the space or the security to let things take their course. They were poised ready for disaster, wishing to 'jump the life to come' (Macbeth).

The replacement child, while fearful and questioning their own right to exist, can, from my clinical experience, also be reckless and full of rage. The varying descriptions of James Joyce encapsulate these extremes: 'courteous' and 'shy', yet set on revenge—the 'injustice collector'. It is a confusing picture, just as being a replacement child is confusing: is one very precious or a usurper; should one hide or assert one's place in the world. It is a tragedy for the mother who loses a child that, in her grief, she can then become the object of the surviving child's rage.

In the first three chapters of *Ulysses,* negative feminine images abound. In the words of Hershey: 'Unable to grieve, locked in the grip of his morbid preoccupations, dispossessed, and wracked with guilt, Stephen walks through Dublin as in a nightmare'. An old milkwoman is noted for her 'old shrunken paps' and 'unclean loins, of man's flesh made not in God's likeness'. She is the 'witch on her toadstool' and the 'old sow that eats her farrow'. The sea, another maternal image, is foul and green (1985, p. 224).

It is hard to think of comparable examples in the literature where such language is used. We see the hatred of women and mothers doing terrible things, but not such condemnation, and so soon after her death. This is Hamlet to his mother, Gertrude, but her betrayal had been more blatant:

> What devil was't
> That thus hath cozen'd you at hoodman-blind?
> Eyes without feeling, feeling without sight,
> Ears without hands or eyes, smelling sans all,
> Could not so mope.
> O Shame! Where is thy blush?
>   (Act iii, iv)

Donald Silver sees the 'Dark Lady' sonnets as Shakespeare's plea to his mother who, having lost three daughters, turned away from him in her grief. Silver says that in Sonnet 143, 'it is not difficult to imagine the boy Shakespeare speaking poignantly from within himself to the mother of his past who mourned to the point of neglecting her eldest son…the sonnet could be entitled 'Ode to a Replacement Child' because it so tellingly depicts the fate of such a child':

> …So runn'st thou after that which flies from thee,
> Whilst I thy babe chase thee afar behind,
> But if thou catch thy hope, turn back to me,
> And play the mother's part, kiss me, be kind.
> So will I pray that thou mayst have thy Will
> If thou turn back, and my loud crying still.
>   (Silver, 1983, p. 525)

A poem of Joyce's has a similar quality and includes the lines:

> Of the dark past
> A child is born,
> With joy and grief
> My heart is torn.
>   [from Ecce Puer]

Shakespeare's *The Winter's Tale* not only has the paranoid and jealous king, Leontes, who feels usurped by his best friend and his son but, when the son dies, Hermione the queen turns to stone—becoming the ultimate 'dead mother'.

Joyce's great friend, Samuel Beckett, not a replacement child and more oppressed than betrayed by his controlling mother, modelled his first novel, *Molloy*, on *Ulysses*. George McIver Steele writes:

> The hatred and contempt which Molloy feels for his mother reach a peak in the same passages in which he writes of taking the key to her strongbox. He calls her 'Countess Caca', describes her 'few niggardly wetted goat-droppings', her 'shrunken hairy old face' and communicates with her by means of 'one or more (according to my needs) thumps of the fist, on her skull'.
>
> (1989, p. 16)

One of Joyce's heroes, William Blake, was, like Joyce, born after the death of a firstborn son. But his mother favoured the next son who was given the dead son's name, John—called 'the evil one', by Blake. As I describe in the *Appendix*, for Blake, mothers were to be feared.

Joyce described his mother's actual death as a 'wound on the brain'. Words became 'the sea crashing in on his breaking brain'. 'Mother, words and sea become inseparable' (O'Brien, 1999, p. 170). This could be a description of his writings. Most memorably, it is the way he ends *Finnegans Wake*. The mother, Anna Livia Plurabelle, is finally given a voice— the dead mother is brought to life and becomes one with the sea:

> 'A way a lone a lost a last a loved a long the'

In the next chapter, I look at Joyce's relationship with his disturbed but beloved father, John Stanislaus Joyce, and question whether the father, too, experienced a 'dead mother' in childhood.

References

Adiv-Ginach, M. (2006). Analysis of a Narcissistic Wound: Reflections on Andre Green's 'The Dead Mother', *Modern Psychoanalysis*, 31(1): 45–57.

Anderson, M. (1990). 'James Joyce in Paris', in E. H. Mikhail, ed., *James Joyce: Interviews and Recollections*. London: Macmillan Press, pp. 133–213.

Britton, R. (1989). *The Oedipus Complex Today: Clinical Implications*. London: Karnac.

Deutsch, H. in Silver, D. (1983). The Dark Lady: Sibling Loss and Mourning in the Shakespearean Sonnets, *Psychoanalytic Inquiry*, 3(3): 513–527.

Ellmann, R. (1982). *James Joyce*, first revised edition of the 1959 classic. Oxford: Oxford University Press.

Enright, A. (2007). *The Gathering*. London: Jonathan Cape.

Frank, N. (1979). 'The Shadow That Had Lost Its Man', in W. Potts & N. Frank, eds., *Portraits of the Artist in Exile. Recollections of James Joyce by Europeans*. Seattle: University of Washington Press, pp. 74–105.

Gerson, S. (2009). When the Third Is Dead: Memory, Mourning, and Witnessing in the Aftermath of the Holocaust, *International Journal of Psychoanalysis*, 90: 1341–1357.

Green, A. (1986). *On Private Madness*. London: Hogarth Press.

Hershey, D. W. (1985). Conflict and Reconciliation in James Joyce's *Ulysses*, *Psychoanalysis and Contemporary Thought*, 8(2): 221–251.

Joyce, J. (1922). *Ulysses*. London: The Bodley Hea.

Joyce, J. (2000). *A Portrait of the Artist as a Young Man*. Ed. Seamus Deane. Harmondsworth, Middlesex: Penguin Books.Joyce, J. (2012). *Finnegans Wake*. Oxford World Classics, OUP.

Kiberd, D. (1992). Introduction: James Joyce, *Ulysses, Annotated Student Edition*. Penguin, pp. ix–lxxx, London.

Meltzer, D. (1967). *The Psycho-Analytical Process*. London: Heinemann; reprinted Strath Tay: Clunie Press, 1970.

O'Brien, E. (1999). *James Joyce*. London: Weidenfeld & Nicolson.

Paige, L. R. (1995). James Joyce's darkly colored portraits of "Mother" in Dubliners, *Studies in Short Fiction*; Newberry, 32(3), (Summer 1995): 329–340.

Power, A. (1990). 'Memoir of the Man', in E. H. Mikhail, ed., *James Joyce: Interviews & Recollections*. Macmillan Press, London, pp. 172–174.

Reid, M. (1992). 'Joshua—Life after Death. The Replacement Child', *Journal of Child Psychotherapy*, 18(2): 109–138.

Silver, D. (1983). The Dark Lady: Sibling Loss and Mourning in the Shakespearean Sonnets, *Psychoanalytic Inquiry*, 3(3): 513–527.

Steele, G. M. (1989). Restoring Silence: Samuel Beckett's 'Molloy' Viewed as a Parody of James Joyce's 'Ulysses', College of William & Mary—Arts & Sciences.

Storey, D. (2021). *A Stinging Delight. David Story: A Memoir*. London: Faber & Faber.

4   *Joyce's Father—The Only Child*. The only son of an only son of an only son

James Joyce's father, John Stanislaus Joyce, born in 1849, was the only son of an only son of an only son. This would have been highly unusual in Catholic Ireland. His father's biographers, Jackson and Costello, suggest that all was not well in the marriages but, given the high rate of childhood deaths, one would be inclined to wonder if they had lost children. Joyce's father, for all his popularity and talent, was seriously disturbed. He became alcoholic, was unable to hold down a job and was frighteningly abusive with his family. As the only son of a well-to-do family, was he, like James, perhaps a replacement child? Was he bearing the weight of grief passed down through the three generations who only had one child each? The biographers, Jackson and Costello (1997), wonder why John Joyce wasn't called after his own father, James. They question was he, too, really a second son, and had his elder brother died? This is their description of Joyce's parents' loss:

> On 23 Nov 1880, …the Joyce's first child was born. To John's delight, it was a boy, like every Joyce child for the previous three generations… The baby was sickly when he was born and, after only eight hopeless days, he died. John was deeply affected by the loss. Years later… John could still say that his life was buried with his son. John Augustine Joyce…had been his 'firstborn and first-fruit of woe'. … In the secret back of his father's mind, Jim had usurped the cot of his dead elder brother. The feeling that his new son was a substitute was never to be admitted.
>
> (1997, pp. 99–113)

The Irish Famine

Surprisingly, in the biography of Joyce's father, there is no discussion of the Irish Famine, even though Joyce's extended family was a big

DOI: 10.4324/9781003309925-5

presence in County Cork and it would have affected them deeply. Joyce's grandfather was born in 1827 and would have been 18 at the time of the Famine in 1845. Joyce's father was born in 1849. Even when Joyce himself was born, in 1882, Ireland would still have been reeling from the Famine. The grandfather turned to drink and died in 1866 when only 39. In Chapter 9, I discuss the Famine as a backdrop to *Ulysses*.

Joyce saw aspects of himself in his father, in both the good and the destructive ways. He told Louis Gillet: 'The humour of *Ulysses* is his; its people are his friends. The book is his spittin' image'. He would rescue his father (and indeed himself) in his writing. As Colm Toibin has described, Joyce may have left his father in Dublin, but he is kept alive, most poetically, in both *Ulysses* and *Finnegans Wake*:

> Since his father's presence loomed so large in the city, Joyce needed to go away so that the man who had begotten him could move into shadow. It was only then that the father could be reimagined and reinvoked in the son's work.
>
> Joyce now sought to outsoar his father, to see him as if through sweetened air from high above: he is Icarus, the son of Daedalus, but an Icarus who will fly to avoid what seeks to ensnare him. As he flies, however, his father always follows. Simon Dedalus appears or is mentioned in seven of the 18 episodes of *Ulysses*.
>
> (2018)

When his father died, aged 80, Joyce sank 'into a Lear-like state of lamentation, blaming himself for a decade of near neglect and occasional outbursts of cruelty'. He was 'reduced to a state of wounded infant-like despair' (O'Brien, 1999, pp. 151–152). On 17 January 1932, Joyce wrote to Harriet Weaver:

> Thanks for your message of sympathy....The weeks since then have been passed in prostration of mind. ...I am thinking of abandoning work altogether...Why go on writing about a place I did not dare to go to at such a moment, where not three persons know me or understand me.
>
> My father had an extraordinary affection for me. He was the silliest man I ever knew and yet cruelly shrewd. He thought and talked of me up to his last breath. I was very fond of him always, being a sinner myself, and even liked his faults. Hundreds of pages and scores of characters in my books came from him. His dry (or rather wet) wit and his expression of face convulsed me often with

laughter. ...I got from him his portraits, a waistcoat, a good tenor voice, and an extravagant licentious disposition (out of which, however, the greater part of any talent I may have springs) but, apart from these, something else I cannot define. ...I thought he would live longer. It is not his death that crushed me so much but self-accusation.

(*SL*, pp. 360–361)

In *A Portrait of the Artist as a Young Man*, Stephen Dedalus describes his father, Simon, as having been a

medical student, an oarsman, a tenor, an amateur actor, a shouting politician, a small landlord, a small investor, a drinker, a good fellow, a storyteller, somebody's secretary, something in a distillery, a taxgatherer, a bankrupt and at present a praiser of his own past.

(*P*, p. 262)

He was an encyclopaedia of Dublin lore and legend and, in taking long walks with him (similar to Freud and his father), Joyce developed his intimate, microscopic appreciation of the 'Dublin experience'.

Finnegans Wake seems a love letter to Joyce's father. 'HCE' becomes the central character, a father of three, who suffers the great fall of Man/Humpty Dumpty. All his possible misdemeanours are considered, he is treated gently and excused, not condemned.

Unlike his brother Stanislaus, James was sent to boarding school and spared some of his father's worst behaviour. After leaving Dublin, Joyce wrote regularly, but never managed to return to see him or have his father visit. About Dublin he said, 'I am attached to it daily and nightly like an umbilical cord'. He confided in T. S. Eliot, who, like Joyce, had escaped into exile, disappointing his own father:

He had an intense love for me and it adds anew to my grief and remorse that I did not go to Dublin to see him for so many years. I kept him constantly under the illusion that I would come and was always in correspondence with him but an instinct I believed in held me back from going, much as I longed to.

(Toibin, 2018)

'Foetus' Vision in 'Portrait of an Artist'

There is an unsettling section in *Portrait*, when he is visiting his old school with his father, where the word *Foetus*, carved in a desktop, triggers a disturbing vision in Stephen of a 'frowning, broadshouldered, moustachioed student' turning on him:

> It shocked him to find in the outer world a trace of what he had deemed till then a brutish and individual malady of his own mind. It made him loathe himself for his own mad and filthy orgies.
>
> (*P*, p. 95)

This episode has understandably been linked to Joyce frequenting brothels. It was also written after his wife had a miscarriage in 1908. But the image of being turned on by this large presence of a frowning student also makes one think of the accusing 'lost brother'.

On one of Joyce's last visits to his father, in 1909, after a walk that ended in a village pub, John Stanislaus Joyce sat down at a piano and played the impassioned aria from the father/son struggle in the third act of *La Traviata*. This is a heart-wrenching aria, especially for a father and son who had been apart, but Joyce seems not to have reacted. Was he angry with his father? Did it come too close to his own feelings of guilt? When leaving the pub, his father asked, 'Did you recognize the aria?' and Joyce replied, 'Yes, it belongs to the father in Verdi's opera' (Gillet, 1979, p. 190). In the aria the father sings:

> What pain your old father has suffered!
> With you away
> His home has been desolate indeed.
> But if in finding you again
> My hopes are not in vain,
> If the voice of honour
> Is not silent for you,
> God has heard me!

One can hardly imagine what was going on for Joyce, confronted with this expression of his father's pain. Did he weep when he recounted this to his close friend, Louis Gillet?

Both Joyce and his father had beautiful tenor voices. In *Ulysses*, in the musical *Sirens* episode which is structured like a fugue, the father, Simon Dedalus, sings *M'appari* (Martha) which is remarkably like the Traviata aria. Bloom says:

> Alas! The voice rose, sighing, changed: loud, full, shining, proud.
> - But alas, 'twas idle dreaming …
> Glorious tone he has still. Cork air softer also their brogue.

Jacques Lacan's famous 1975 'Le Sinthome' seminar was on Joyce's struggle with his father, focusing on the paternal function (see also Cox, 1993). Lacan talks in terms of Joyce's father having 'failed' him. He sees Joyce gradually creating a sustaining father internally through his writing. But Joyce felt he, too, had failed his father and his writing seems a form of reparation. The death of the first son was an impossible reality for both.

Joyce's father's death coincided with the birth of his grandson for which he wrote the poem, *Ecce Puer*, which ends:

> Young life is breathed
> On the glass;
> The world that was not
> Comes to pass.
> A child is sleeping:
> An old man gone.
> O, father forsaken,
> Forgive your son!
> (*JJ*, p. 646)

References

Cox, O. (1993). Some Dream Mechanisms in Finnegans Wake, *International Journal of Psycho-Analysis*, 74: 815–821.

Ellmann, R. (1982). *James Joyce*. Oxford: Oxford University Press.

Ellmann, R., ed. (1992). *Selected Letters of James Joyce*. London: Faber and Faber.

Gillet, L. (1979). 'The Living Joyce', in W. Potts, ed., *Portraits of the Artist in Exile. Recollections of James Joyce by Europeans*. Seattle: University of Washington Press, pp. 170–204.

Jackson, J. W., & Costello, P. (1997). *John Stanislaus Joyce: The Voluminous Life and Genius of James Joyce's Father*. London: Fourth Estate.

Joyce, J. (2000). *A Portrait of the Artist as a Young Man*. London: Penguin Modern Classics.

Lacan, J. (1974–75). RSI. Séminaire. Cesbron-Lavau, H. (ed.). Paris: Éditions de l'Association Lacanienne Internationale.

O'Brien, E. (1999). *James Joyce*. London: Weidenfeld & Nicolson.

Toibin, C. (2018). His Spittin' Image, *London Review of Books*, 40(4). 22 February.

5 Guilt and Persecution. Intrusive identification and the world of the claustrum

There are sins or (let us call them as the world calls them) evil memories which are hidden away by man in the darkest places of the heart but they abide there and wait. ...Yet a chance word will call them forth suddenly and they will rise up to confront him in the most various circumstances, a vision or a dream.

(*U*, p. 552)

The Claustrum—'A Paradise of Paranoia'

Ulysses begins with usurpers, guilt and condemnation in the womb-like Martello Tower. Stephen Dedalus is down inside while Buck Mulligan is urging him to 'leave the moody brooding' and 'come up into the sweet air'. Joyce, 'exiled in on himself', seemed ensconced in what Donald Meltzer described as a claustrum world. The claustrum is a difficult concept because of the literalness with which Meltzer talks about being inside the internal mother. Margaret Rustin calls it a most useful concept: 'I find myself explaining his theory to bewildered therapists who are suffering the experience of being with a child who seems inside something, while they remain irrelevant outsiders' (2017, p. 14).

Meltzer's 'claustrum' is an internal world full of condemnation, betrayal and fear—a Kafkaesque prison with no way out. Persecution plagued Joyce and pervades *Ulysses*. Marilyn French describes the *Circe* section of *Ulysses* as 'a paradise of paranoia':

The chapter is like a medieval last judgment, in which everything in the hierarchical universe, from the pebbles and sand at its bottom to the souls and angels near its top, arises to accuse man. Everything joins forces to hound our heroes.

(1988, p. 186)

DOI: 10.4324/9781003309925-6

Joyce spent his life trying to understand his inner 'daimons'. He was 'ruled, roped, duped and driven by those numen daimons, the feekeepers at their laws, nightly consternation' (FW). Immersing himself in Freud, especially *The Interpretation of Dreams*, he tried to analyse his nightmares but, to understand his early trauma, he would have needed Melanie Klein's descriptions of the child's internal world and Andre Green's concept of the 'dead mother'.

Melanie Klein had the extraordinary ability to enter into the world of very young children. She described the infant wanting to 'force its way into the mother's body in order to take possession of the contents and to destroy them, it wants to know what is going on and what things look like in there' (1932, p. 241). Donald Meltzer expanded on Klein's discovery by dividing the inner space of the mother into three geographical compartments: the head, the breast and the genitals. 'My contribution', he said, 'consisted of an invasion of a space that is really a mythological space—the unconscious'. His theory brought to life the persecutory world of the claustrum:

> Because projective identification is essentially an intrusion, the essential atmosphere of the mental life of the part that has intruded into the object is that it is a trespasser, that it is in disguise, that it does not belong there, and is therefore always in danger of being revealed as an interloper. That is the most essential factor in the nature of claustrophobia, the constant danger of being revealed as an interloper.
>
> (Meltzer, 1992)

One can hear how this resonates with the world of the replacement child—an interloper who does not belong there, a dynamic played out in the Martello Tower at the start of *Ulysses*.

The book has 18 sections, each one linked to a body part, and the three main characters seem located in the compartments of the mother's body: Stephen Dedalus, the poet-artist, is located in the head-breast (Meltzer's 'Lotus Eaters' lassitude); Molly Bloom, fantasising in bed with 'compulsive greed for sexual stimulation', is located in the genital compartment; and Leopold Bloom is in the anal world of the rectum.

This is Meltzer's description of life in the maternal rectum:

> Seen from the inside, intruded by stealth or violence…it is a region of satanic religion… the world of Orwell's 'Big Brother'.
>
> Truth is transformed into anything that cannot be disproved… all the acts of intimacy change their meaning into techniques of

manipulation… loyalty replaces devotion; obedience substitutes for trust; emotion is simulated by excitement; guilt and the yearning for punishment takes the place of regret.

There is only one value: survival. The nameless dread consists in being 'thrown away'. This nameless dread is exponentially worse even than exile: it is absolute loneliness.

(1992, pp. 91–92)

It is a world empty of maternal comfort or reassurance.

The rectal compartment is described by Meltzer as being not only a place of claustrophobic anxieties, 'it's the place of perversions, it's the place of drug addictions, it's a place of criminality and sadomasochism of all sorts' (1992, p. 120). Joyce's anal preoccupation is well documented and seen especially in his correspondence with his wife Nora.

A dream that Joyce had in 1922 at the age of 40 has all the dread and inevitability of the claustrum. It is located inside a 'luscious Persian pavilion', like the inside of the mother:

> There were sixteen rooms, four on each floor. Someone had committed a crime, and he entered the lowest floor. The door opened on a flower garden. He hoped to get through but when he arrived at the threshold a drop of blood fell on it. *I could know* how desperate he felt, for he went from the first floor all the way up to the fourth, his hope being that at each threshold his wound was not capable of letting fall another drop. *But always it came,* an official discovered it, and punctually at the sixteen rooms the drop fell. There were two officials in brocaded silk robes, and a man with a scimitar who watched him.

Joyce, in his self-analysis, interpreted the rooms as the 12 signs of the zodiac, the three doors are the Trinity, the man who committed the crime was himself, and the man with the scimitar was his 'wife next morning'. The pavilion with light blue lattices was 'like a box', he said (*JJ*, p. 547). We do not know the context for this dream, except that he had seen the Russian ballet the night before and was writing *Finnegans Wake*, but as well as a 'criminal' entering the lowest floor (the rectal compartment) trying to evade being discovered, there is a distinct sense of nameless dread and 'ineluctability', meaning inevitable and inescapable, which has the ring of proleptic certainty, such as I describe in the next chapter: 'I could always know' and 'always it came'. Most poignantly the man in the dream was wounded and felt desperate with no way of escape.

Edna O'Brien describes Joyce's dreams as 'more like the unconscious trajectory of Kafka than of Joyce' (1999, p. 169). In the dream,
the desperate wish to 'escape' from some obscure guilt, and getting
stuck instead in some luscious palace with erotic overtones, gives a
glimpse of the state of mind in which Joyce wrote *Ulysses*. The dream,
however, pales in comparison with the wild nightmarish pantomime
Circe section. It seems as though it is this escape into madness/pathos/
humour that helped free Joyce from the Kafkaesque prison. In *Circe*,
lonely Bloom is hauled before a court judge and accused of everything
under the sun in front of a baying mob. It is the extended heartfelt
outcry of someone caught in the bogus persecutory world of the claustrum. It is a world replete with all kinds of 'sluts and ragamuffins',
bishops and ghosts and a seductive Molly Bloom *'in Turkish costume,
her opulent curves filling out the scarlet trousers and jacket slashed with gold'*
(U, 570). Stephen's dead mother also appears, as do Macbeth and the
three witches (U, 682). As I describe in Chapter 7, there is another
courtroom scene in *Finnegans Wake*. Making fun of judge, jury and
all involved seems for Joyce a brilliant and effective strike against the
inner persecutory 'gang'.

Intrusive Identification

It is not surprising that a child, faced with a grieving mother, might
try to get right inside, to get a foothold somewhere and become one
with her. This is what Meltzer calls *intrusive identification*, as opposed to
identifying with the mother as a separate person. This kind of intrusion
becomes imprisoning for the child and any separation is like an expul-
sion into the void. In psychoanalysis, we sometimes sense that patients
are right inside us. This dynamic became overwhelming with one of
my patients. Having to wait outside in the waiting room she found
unbearable and she would rush into the consulting room. At the end
of each session, she felt 'thrust out' and would flee before I could say
it was time. In an early dream she was being invited to play a musical
instrument:

> It was a combined instrument, half harpsichord, half viol, at differ-
> ent angles facing away from each other and a deep red colour. One
> side was alive and like a dragon, and the other inanimate. To play it
> you had to *get right inside* it. It seemed impossible to play.

Her difficulties getting inside me and 'playing' me frustrated her. She
tried from all different angles and she expressed fury at these mothers

who won't let her in. The two sides of the instrument seemed a picture of her only alternatives as either being wild like a dragon or silenced and lying low.

She brought poems *to* me and *about* me, seductive in their skill. I was a *wiry witch* in a difficult to enter or manipulate box. There are images of 'portals of entry', getting through the double doors: *Outside the door I wait for clouds to crack...*; into my shoes: *Her shoes are small and flat and black, like loss....*; my eyes: *Her eyes are Meissen blue: she can't command them. They bite and dance....* Then she has me '*thrusting*' her out. At the same time there was the wish to make us the same, both mothers, for example, and knowing the same, reading Melanie Klein, to avoid our separateness and having to imagine herself in my shoes—or even put herself in her own shoes, so to speak, and feel compassion for herself rather than guilt.

Her imagination is given a kind of free rein but with a purpose to control and express her love and fury. What was less free about her imagination was the ability to imagine alternatives and risk having her anger collapse into grief.

Survivor Guilt

'Survivor guilt' in the replacement child can produce accusation and self-blame in the child's imagination. My patients were convinced of their badness due to their envious fantasies and they were obsessed with guilt feelings. But this was not depressive position guilt seeking forgiveness. They didn't expect or even seek compassion in life, only condemnation. Feelings they had were intense and hard to control and often produced behaviour that one might well condemn. It was as though they wanted to prove their badness, but any attempt by me to address this seemed to touch on real fragility and fear.

Ulysses is full of similar outpouring, getting revenge on the many people Joyce felt had wronged him. This is a classic example of projective identification since, as a young man, Joyce himself was notorious for offending people. Leon Edel called Joyce an 'Injustice Collector', and Hugh Kenner points out that Joyce imprisoned himself and had to remain in exile because of all the lawsuits he would have had against him had he returned to Ireland: 'Joyce's revenge on Oliver Gogarty [Buck Mulligan in the book] was to shut him into a book for all to see whenever they care to' (Kenner, 1962, p. 49).

In *Ulysses*, Leopold Bloom as a character seems quite extraordinarily strange. Joyce tries to lift him into a realm of great humanity, saintliness even, as though this 'womanly man' might be the ideal. But at the same time he is portraying a grieving, cuckolded, marginalised Jew who distracts himself with endless bits of information, and inhabits a world of masturbation. Joyce, thinking of his parents' loss, may want to save this bereaved couple, Molly and Bloom, who lost a child, and bring them to life again. But it doesn't happen. At the end, they remain lying topsy turvy with Bloom kissing Molly's buttocks, unable to overcome their grief. Stephen fled from becoming their replacement son.

In real life, Joyce's sense of entitlement—born of fear and a reversal of guilt feelings—particularly with his wife and brother, made him notoriously ruthless. It is a curious dynamic with some who lost siblings how they latch onto another sibling in a most intense and controlling way, creating a sado-masochistic *folie a deux*. Van Gogh was a famous example. Stephen Spender describes Joyce's brother, Stanislaus, as playing the role of an alter ego to the writer: 'occasionally giving him a slap, but far more often only standing there to be knocked down and robbed (metaphorically) of his pants, which Joyce then puts on' (1966). A letter from Joyce's brother on his return to Trieste, after having been interned for four years in an Austrian camp, conveys how fed up he was with Joyce's treatment of him.

> I have just emerged from four years of hunger and squalor, and am trying to get on my feet again. Do you think you can give me a rest?
> (McCourt, 2000, p. 249)

But Joyce couldn't and didn't.

It is as though the fear and anger associated with the survivor guilt of the 'replacement child' become so unbearable that the only escape is to actually *be* bad, 'break all the windows' (Woolf), and enter the world finally in their rightful place, as a criminal, achieving a perverse kind of authenticity.

At the same time, Joyce, like my patients, could be very good company and with his brilliant mind and wit he was funny and seductive. According to his biographer, 'no one could laugh more wholeheartedly or more infectiously'. With his head back and mouth wide, he resounded throughout the room, and he was always bursting into song. Another image is of him doing his spider dance down the street—his long legs flailing around (*JJ*, 430). His many admirers went out of their way for him. Meltzer refers to this 'mysterious charisma' that paralyses the opposition—especially the loved ones. Joyce's wife, tested to the limit with his late-night drinking and problems with money, stood by him devotedly and lovingly, like a mother, tuned in to his fears and vulnerability.

The lively and seductive qualities in both of my patients seemed partly to be ways of trying to lodge inside and be as one with me rather than engaging as separate people and developing the kind of intercourse in which play and trust could develop. They seemed to take over sessions and fill the space, almost as though they were 'killing me off', the way they felt killed off, and which perhaps reinforces their belief that they are lethal. Joyce's (half-joking) comment that the demand he makes of his reader is that he should 'devote his whole life to reading my works', has a similar feel to it (*JJ*, 703).

Escaping the Claustrum

Although throughout his life Joyce seemed prone to fear, it is impressive how, through his writing, he was able to create for himself a world of connection, forgiveness and humour. Physically leaving Dublin must have been essential for Joyce, but escaping a persecutory internal world is of a different order. Meltzer describes the analyst's difficulty persuading patients out of the claustrum, 'up into the sweet air', given the narcissism and lack of trust. Emerging from an isolated paranoid–schizoid state can produce intense emotions including painful regrets as well as new joy.

Joyce wrote *Ulysses* in a state of grief and dislocation adjusting to his new life in exile. Absorbed in his writing, he could give voice to his emotional state and it seemed to release him. As I describe in Chapter 11, this created a shift in Joyce and an escape from the paranoid–schizoid to a depressive position embrace of the world.

As his friend, Thomas McGreevey, wrote in 1932 when Joyce was 50 and in the middle of *Finnegans Wake*:

> He writes about human beings as the most enlightened and humane of father confessors might, if it were permitted, write about his penitents. For an Irish Catholic, his Dublin is the eternal Dublin, as Dante's Florence is the eternal Florence, Dublin meditated on, crooned over, laughed at, loved, warned, Dublin with its moments of hope and its almost perpetual despair, its boastfulness and its cravenness, its nationalism, its provincialism, its religion, its profanity, its Sunday mornings, its Saturday nights, its culture, its ignorance, its work, its play, its streets, its lanes, its port, its parks, its statues; its very cobbles, and the feet, shod and unshod, worthy and unworthy—if a charity like Joyce's permits the use of so final a word as 'unworthy' in relation to any human being—that walk them.
>
> (Mikhail, 1990, p. 142)

Joyce's great capacity for observation, deep thought and experimentation seems to have allowed him also to play and saved him from the paranoid world of his youth.

References

Ellmann, R. ed. (1975). *Selected Letters of James Joyce.* London: Faber & Faber.

Ellmann, R. (1982). *James Joyce*, first revised edition of the 1959 classic. Oxford: Oxford University Press.

French, M. (1988). *The Book as World. James Joyce's Ulysses.* New York: [Paragon House] Abacus.

Joyce, J. (1960/80). *Ulysses.* London: Bodley Head.

Kenner, H. (1962). *Flaubert, Joyce and Beckett: The Stoic Comedians.* London: Dalkey Archive Press.

Klein, M. (1932). *The Psycho-Analysis of Children. The Writings of Melanie Klein Vol. 2.* London Hogarth Press, 1975; reprinted London: Karnac, 1993.

McCourt, J. (2000). *The Years of Bloom. James Joyce in Trieste, 1904–1920.* Dublin: Lilliput Press.

McGreevey, T. (1990). 'Homage to James Joyce', in E. H. Mikhail, ed., *James Joyce: Interviews & Recollections.* Macmillan Press, p. 142.

Meltzer, D. (1992). *The Claustrum: An Investigation of Claustrophobic Phenomena.* Strath Tay: Clunie Press.

Rustin, M. (2017). 'Doing Things Differently: An Appreciation of Donald Meltzer's Contribution', in M. Cohen & A. Hahn, eds., *Doing Things Differently. The Influence of Donald Meltzer on Psychoanalytic Practice.* London: Karnac, pp. 5–20.

Spender, S. (1966). 'Self-Portrait of the Artist', *Letters of James Joyce, Vols. 2 and 3*, R. Ellmann, ed., *NYTimes* December.

6 *Imagination vs Fantasy.* The Ineluctability of the Proleptic Imagination

Good old Coleridge would call that fancy, not imagination.

Joyce

The function of the imagination is not to make strange things settled, so much as to make settled things strange.

Chesterton

James Joyce questioned whether he had a 'pure imagination'.

In a state of doubt and worry, Joyce referred to it several times. Because of it, all of his efforts were accompanied by a feeling of malaise.

(Mercanton, 1979, 224)

On the face of it, this seems a strange concern from the man who wrote *Ulysses* and *Finnegans Wake*. But it is, in fact, a question that goes to the heart of work with traumatised patients whose memories and imagination can perpetuate their fears. As a highly sensitive child with 'an overabundance of imagination' (Bloom), much of it persecutory, Joyce needed to manage and channel his thoughts. Although both *Ulysses* and *Finnegans Wake* are highly imaginative and creative, they were written within a meticulously controlled structure.

Freeing one's thoughts and imagination is a core developmental task and key in the work of psychoanalysis. It is particularly difficult for the traumatised patient. Joyce used his exceptional memory and brilliant intellect to hold together emotionally, but internally he was under constant threat, 'a paper leaf away from madness'. His well-known terror

DOI: 10.4324/9781003309925-7

of thunderstorms seems symbolic of his susceptibility to disintegration. Franco Bruni witnessed Joyce's fear:

> A sort of hysterical man with a morbid hypersensitivity, he was insanely frightened by electrical storms...Overcome by terror, he would clap his hands over his ears, run and hide in a small darkened room or hurl himself into bed in order not to see or hear.
>
> (1979, p. 46)

Thunder is the image of an outside threat that could happen at any time and upset his equilibrium.

The biographer, Richard Ellmann, said Joyce's writing involved 'the imaginative absorption of stray material. The method did not please Joyce very much because he considered it not imaginative enough, but it was the only way he could work' (*JJ*, p. 250). Similarly, his friend Arthur Power described Joyce as 'a realist, determined to see, accept and write about things exactly as they are. His work is based on memory, rather than imagination' (1990, p. 173).

Having spent his life recalling, re-imagining and revising his memories of Dublin, his writing emerges from actual scenes, historical facts and general encyclopaedic knowledge. 'He was never a creator *ex nihilo*; he recomposed what he remembered, and he remembered most of what he had seen or had heard other people remember' (*JJ*, p. 364). His was a memory that retained everything he saw and heard.

I am looking at the distinction between a controlled 'proleptic' imagination which provides a sense of certainty, and a playful free imagination. This distinction has long intrigued writers and critics and is expressed in Keats's 'negative capability'—the ability of the creative poet to allow uncertainty and use intuition and identification. The important distinction is between the two types of identification: imaginative and intrusive. *Intrusive* identification operates to avoid uncertainty and the unexpected by eliminating the freedom and separateness of the other. *Imaginative* identification opens the mind to new possibilities and realities. Hazlitt is quoted by Bate as saying:

> Shakespeare... could take any form, and could negate his own identity in that of any other person, and follow out 'the germs of every faculty and feeling...intuitively, into all their conceivable ramifications, through every change of fortune, or conflict of passion. *He had only to think of anything in order to become that thing, with all the circumstances belonging to it*'.
>
> (1982)

'Becoming' that thing still allows its otherness. Margot Waddell describes how George Eliot recognised the distinction:

> It is an insight into the nature of the difference between, on the one hand, the imitation of external reality and the manipulative controlling of it, and on the other, the imbuing of it with meaning, culled from the joys and pains of the experience of the external world. This insight lies at the heart of the novels—the relationship between George Eliot's method of realism and her deeper meanings.
>
> (1986, p. 114)

Perhaps by closely observing the pain of experience, for example, Joyce was increasingly able to allow distance and uncertainty and imbue his writing with meaning and portray with humour the prison of a Kafkaesque, claustrum world. As in psychoanalysis, his writing gave him a place to articulate and externalise his inner turmoil. It is impressive to see the transformation and greater imaginative freedom in him. Perhaps by placing *Finnegans Wake* in the night-time dreamworld, Joyce had found a way to control the dreams that plagued him. His self-reproach becomes externalised into his characters where his guilt can be mocked, puzzled over and ultimately forgiven. In *Ulysses*, he seems still personally immersed in the pain of his characters. As John Banville asks: 'What happened to Joyce in those *Wanderjahre*? How was the precious young man who had set out to "forge the conscience of my race" enabled to find within himself that tremendous humanistic and comic gift?' (1999) His friend, Gerald Griffin, described a more overall change in him:

> That is Joyce as he is now—tolerant of all criticism, confident that he is right, yet sensitive to the last degree. The truculent, almost swashbuckling, hard-swearing, seedy-looking young Dubliner has merged into the mellow, genial, quiet, well-dressed man of poise and distinction. Aloof and frigid to gate-crashing journalists, he is the soul of hospitality and generosity to his personal friends.
>
> (1990, p. 153)

For the traumatised child, controlling the imagination is paramount. Holocaust survivors who saw sights beyond imagination needed to block the real images from their minds (Grubrich-Simitis, 1984). The replacement child who feels to blame for a sibling's death has a similar but somewhat different task. Although in both cases there will be survivor guilt, the replacement child may fear retribution. In 'Terror,

Persecution, and Dread', Meltzer (1968) describes an extreme form of paranoid anxiety in infancy:

> The object of terror (being in unconscious phantasy dead objects) cannot even be fled from with success. The mother's internal babies are not only damaged …but killed by the destructive-possessive jealousy. What is feared is the retaliatory re-projection of the murderous attacks on the mother's internal babies.
>
> (Cassese, 1995, p. 43)

The infant's rivalry with and murderous wishes towards mother's other babies are key to understanding the anxiety of the replacement child. Hughes quotes Klein on the child's unconscious phantasies:

> Phantasies of forcing the whole self into the inside of the object (to obtain control and possession) led, through fear of retaliation, to a variety of persecutory anxieties such as claustrophobia, or to such common phobias as burglars, spiders, invasion in wartime.
>
> (1991, p. 31)

'These Deeds Must Not Be Thought'

The images of dead babies and scenes of destruction in the nightmares of my replacement child patients were a constant terror and dread for them. Helping them believe they were not to blame for the sibling's death was hampered by these dreams reinforcing their murderousness. One patient said to me, 'You say I *think* I'm murderous. I *know* I am'. Although this conveyed awareness of the difference between picturing and knowing, part of her really believed she is dangerous. Her interest was in finding out what it is about her that is dangerous to others, what has she done. More difficult was for her to question this belief and to imagine she is *not* dangerous. She even quoted Lady Macbeth: 'These deeds must not be thought, after these ways: so, it will make us mad' (Act 2, scene 2).

In psychoanalysis, helping patients to free their imagination and picture things in different ways requires of them a leap of faith. Grubrich-Simitis describes the need for patients and analysts to first acknowledge the external reality of the trauma, outside of the transference relationship (1984, p. 316). With my patients, this involved persuading them they were not murderers and had not caused the death even if they had harboured death wishes against the sibling. This was slow work as they were caught in a fixed state, convinced of their guilt and badness. They sought safety in concrete thinking: if it was in their dream, it must be true. It was hard for me to take in that these intelligent women could hold so firmly to such a delusional and self-destructive belief.

Much of their self-protection involved hiding and escape, whether by entering the object or other means of refuge. They used alcohol to relieve anxiety and achieve a temporary kind of mindlessness. All his life Joyce escaped into his writing and worked to obscure so much of it. Literally going into exile and moving to a new country, as all three did, seems another attempt to disappear. At home, they were the imposter/usurper. Dublin for Joyce became equated with his inner persecuted state—especially after he gave real cause to alienate Dubliners by parodying them in *Ulysses*. About returning there, Joyce had the fixed idea that someone would shoot him.

The Proleptic Imagination

A proleptic imagination is employed in a state of anxiety and is based on delusional certainty and the fantasy that we can know what will happen. It is something we all use at times of stress and surely plays a part in the arrogance and certainty of youth. But it can become a prison for a traumatised child. If the certainty they adopt is that they are guilty and that there will be a bad outcome, they are trapped in fear waiting for the worst to happen.

Proleptic means a leaping ahead and in the proleptic imagination a world is created in which the patient 'knows' what will happen. It is an unconscious attempt to control the imagination but one that traps one in the deluded state. Fisher describes it as 'whatever is pictured—in the moment as well as in the future—is taken concretely as reality' (2017, p. 92). It differs from Klein's concept of 'symbolic equation' (1930, p. 220) in that it focuses on the role of the imagination and describes an overall state of mind. Symbolic equation refers to a difficulty thinking symbolically. My patients could think symbolically but tried, unconsciously, to control their thinking. Rather than allowing things to take their course, they tell themselves they know what will happen. It is the antithesis of Bion's image of reverie and receptiveness and of being without memory or desire. Based on fantasy, this state of mind works to block the free use of the imagination.

One patient refers to this omnipotent state of mind, which perhaps we should call proleptic fantasy, as her tendency to 'catastrophize', the way she anticipates and 'knows' there will be a disaster of her own causing. So firm was the belief in her murderousness that she quoted a murderer released from prison who asked: "'How can I make a life for myself when I have killed someone?" I know what he means', she said. This is a fearsome state to live in and, tragically, as frightening as living in a state of not knowing. Another time she described encountering a deer when walking down a narrow country lane. In the confrontation, the deer's only option was to jump a barbed wire fence, which it did and was injured. She was badly shaken and said it was another example of how she causes damage wherever she goes, even just going for a country walk. In her mind, it wasn't merely chance and something that could have happened to anyone.

Sabbadini describes the replacement child who lost a sibling as 'treated more as the embodiment of a memory than as a person in its own right'. Being allowed a life of their own was problematic, given their sense that they should not have survived when their siblings had died (1988, p. 530). Desperate to prove their worth, and feeling angry at their situation, can make them very competitive. However, success immediately brings new fears. Whatever survivors do, they feel that being competitive risks caus- ing the demise of the other. Anisfeld and Richards give a description of this dynamic in their paper on the 'replacement child':

> He could never be certain that he was loved for who he was or for the genuineness of his achievements. When he performed an action from which he reaped a reward at someone else's expense, he was convinced that he had initiated it; if his deeds were in any way altru- istic, he doubted their sincerity. He believed that he should have been able to do the impossible and save the lives of his half-sisters *even though he had not yet been born*. This grandiose fantasy paradoxically made him scorn his actual accomplishments as worthless and even led him to be taken advantage of by others for their own glorification.
>
> (2000, p. 314; emphasis added)

Here we get a vivid picture of the patient's proleptic belief system—he believed it *even though he had not yet been born*—and a sense of how impris- oning it can be. Joyce, whose competitiveness was extreme (Trilling, 1967, p. 463), faces the competition head-on, outsmarts everyone, destroys the way things have been done before and is credited with the birth of the modernist novel! As T. S. Eliot put it, 'His book destroyed the whole of the nineteenth century' (Ibid, p. 452).

There seems a similarity between the proleptic imagination and Freud's 'omnipotence of thought'. According to Hamilton:

> In introducing the concept of a death instinct, Freud was attempt- ing to master conflicts related to the omnipotence of thought, and

death wishes in particular, where the wish is taken as the equivalent of the deed, as well as to fears of his own death—his work was begun when Freud was 62, having just passed one of the years, 61, in which he was certain he would die and was preceded by this essay on 'The Uncanny' (1919), where he attempts to explain such mysterious phenomena as being functions of the omnipotence of thought.

(1976, p. 157)

The proleptic is about certainty and implies the unavoidable, the ineluctable. Both Freud and Joyce were drawn to the concept of the 'ineluctable' but, while for Joyce the ineluctable was persecutory and the inevitability of being exposed and condemned, for Freud the ineluctable was death.

Joyce chose the world of the dream for *Finnegans Wake*. Dreams are themselves the proleptic imagination at work producing fantasy images that we experience as reality during the dream. Fisher differentiates between a positive proleptic imagination, which allows us to picture and manage our emotional experience through these images and stories, and a negative proleptic imagination, which becomes a defensive attack on unbearable emotion (2017, p. 92).

It is only when we wake from the dream that we can reflect on the images as an expression of our emotional states. My patients, however, found it difficult to create a distance from their dreams—they felt their dreams were more factual evidence of how dangerous or guilty they were. One patient worried about having unconscious murderous wishes: 'Does this mean I am guilty having such feelings or not?' she asked. We can see in this question her confusion and a switch to the concrete.

Given how much he relied on his prodigious memory, Joyce tried, unsuccessfully, to equate memory and imagination. He was drawn to the philosopher Giambattista Vico's (1725) theory of circularity: 'Imagination is nothing but the springing up again of reminiscences, and ingenuity or invention is nothing but the working over of what is remembered'. But his struggle was with the distinction Coleridge made between Imagination and Fancy (Litz, 1961, pp. 126–127). The psychoanalyst, Thomas Ogden, makes the same distinction:

> The imaginative capacity in the analytic setting is nothing less than sacred. Imagination holds open multiple possibilities experimenting with them all in the form of thinking, playing, dreaming and in every other sort of creative activity. Imagination stands in contrast to fantasy which has a fixed form that is repeated again and again

and goes nowhere.... To imagine is not to figure out a solution to an emotional problem; it is to change the very terms of the dilemma.

(2005, p. 26)

One wonders what 'changing the terms of the dilemma' would be for Joyce. In his writing, he was clearly experimenting with multiple possibilities. While using this to throw the reader off, stay one step ahead, at the same time it gave him a new freedom. Rather than being constrained by the structure he set himself, whether it was Odysseus' journey in *Ulysses* or 'the fall of man' in *Finnegans Wake*, the structure seems to have provided a safety within which he could play, similar to that found in the analytic setting. As Ellmann describes:

In the first episodes [of *Ulysses*] he realized his ambition of rendering the thousand complexities in the mind, and for the first time in literature we have all the lapses and bursts of attention, hesitations, half-recollections, distractions, sudden accesses or flaggings of sexual interest, feelings of hunger or nausea, somnolence, sneezing, thoughts about money, responses to the clouds and sunlight, along with the complications of social behavior and work.

(*JJ*)

Colm Toibin gives the following description:

Joyce was concerned not with some dark vision he had of mankind and our fate in the world but rather with the individual self he named and made in all its particularity and privacy. The self's deep preoccupations, the isolation of the individual consciousness, which keeps so much concealed, were what he wished to dramatise. The self ready to feel fear or remorse, contempt or disloyalty, bravery or timidity; the self in a cage of solitude or in the grip of grim lust; the self ready to notice everything except that there was no escape from the self, or indeed from the dilapidated city; these were his subjects.

(2012, *Guardian*)

Obsessed with Dublin ('Have I ever left?'), he never returned to test his fears, but he longed for news from his fatherland, described by Gillet:

What news? That of his own people. I mean, his rivals, brothers in poetry. He spoke tirelessly of Padraic Colum, Sean O'Casey, and especially of the beloved J M Synge...Many times I heard him recite with admiration the marvellous poem of Yeats: *My impetuous heart, be still! Be still!*

These verses came to his lips like an ever-present echoing of a previous existence. They were his world, his fatherland. He never stopped corresponding with a lot of faithful friends and former college comrades who constituted his secret party, as if he were a pretender in exile.

(1979, p. 185)

Always a brilliant thinker, Joyce's assessment of things was deep and intricate, but somehow not open to question. One knew not to challenge this hypersensitive 'strange and beautiful creature'. In later life, he became happier and more settled. Louis Gillet said Joyce emphasised family affection to an extreme degree:

This terrible nay-sayer was a family man; in the chaos of the universe, as in the Deluge, his family was for him a sheet-anchor, the sacred Ark. He was attached to rites, dates, anniversaries, to a secret calendar to which he ascribed a superstitious importance... for nothing in the world would he miss celebrating, Candlemas, the date of his birth, or his father's.

(1979, p. 181)

In Chapter 11, I describe the new freedom of *Finnegans Wake*—a dream of his own making and very different from the persecutory nightmare. Joyce himself referred to *Finnegans Wake* as having a 'prophetic and magical nature' (*JJ*, p. 525). Perhaps the 'prophetic' is similar to the 'ineluctable' (Joyce's favourite word), which echoes the proleptic imagination and its sense of inevitability. But 'magical' is something else and it may have felt magical in the new freedom it allowed. His wife described the fun he had with it and heard him chuckling to himself as he wrote. *Finnegans Wake* is a world away from the grief and isolation of *Ulysses*.

References

Anisfeld, L., & Richards, A. D. (2000). The Replacement Child: Variations on a Theme in History and Psychoanalysis, *Psychoanalytic Study of the Child*, 55: 301–318.

Banville, J. (1999). The Motherless Child. *New York Review of Books*, December 16.

Bate, W. J. (1982). An Exagmination of Imagination, November 18, *New York Review of Books*.

Bruni, A. F. (1979). 'Recollections of Joyce', in W. Potts, ed., *Portraits of the Artist in Exile. Recollections of James Joyce by Europeans*. Seattle: University of Washington Press, pp. 39–46.

Budgen, F. (1972). *James Joyce and the Making of 'Ulysses'*. Oxford: Oxford UP.

Cassese, S. F. (1995). *Introduction to the Work of Donald Meltzer*. London: Karnac.

Eliot, T. S. (1923). 'Ulysses Order and Myth', in *The Dial*, November 1923.

Ellmann, R. (1982). *James Joyce*, first revised edition of the 1959 classic. Oxford: Oxford University Press.

Fisher, J. V. (2017). The Macbeths in the Consulting Room, S. Nathans & M. Schaefer, eds., *Couples on the Couch. Psychoanalytic Couple Therapy and the Tavistock Model*, London: Routledge, pp. 90–112.

Gillet, L. (1979). 'The Living Joyce', in W. Potts, ed., *Portraits of the Artist in Exile. Recollections of James Joyce by Europeans*. Seattle: University of Washington Press, pp. 163–169.

Griffin, G. (1990). 'James Joyce', in E. H. Mikhail, ed., *James Joyce. Interviews and Recollections*. London: The Macmillan Press, p. 149.

Grubrich-Simitis, I. (1984). From Concretism to Metaphor—Thoughts on Some Theoretical and Technical Aspects of the Psychoanalytic Work with Children of Holocaust Survivors, *The Psychoanalytic Study of the Child*, 39: 301–319.

Hamilton, J. W. (1976). Some Comments about Freud's Conceptualization of the Death Instinct, *International Review of Psycho-Analysis*, 3: 151–164.

Hughes, A. ed. (1991). *The Inner World and Joan Riviere. Collected Papers 1920–1958*. London: Karnac Books.

Klein, M. (1930). The Importance of Symbol Formation in the Development of the Ego, *The International Journal of Psychoanalysis*, 11: 24–39.

Litz, A. W. (1961). *The Art of James Joyce: Method and Design in Ulysses* and *Finnegans Wake*. Oxford: Oxford University Press.

Meltzer, D. (1968). Terror, Persecution, Dread: A Dissection of Paranoid Anxieties, *The International Journal of Psychoanalysis*, 49(2–3): 396–401.

Mercanton, J. (1979). 'The Hours of James Joyce', in W. Potts, ed., (1979). *Portraits of the Artist in Exile. Recollections of James Joyce by Europeans*. Seattle: University of Washington Press, pp. 205–252.

Ogden, T. H. (2005). *This Art of Psychoanalysis: Dreaming Undreamt Dreams and Interrupted Cries*. London: Routledge.

Power, A. (1990). In E. H. Mikhail, ed. *James Joyce: Interviews & Recollections*. Macmillan Press.

Sabbadini, A. (1988). The Replacement Child, *Contemporary Psychoanalysis*, 24: 528–547.

Toibin, C. (2012). Joyce's Dublin: City of Dreamers and Chancers, *Guardian*, June.

Trilling, L. (1967). James Joyce in his letters, *The Moral Obligation to be Intelligent: Selected Essays*. Evanston, IL: Northwestern University Press, pp. 450–476.

Waddell, M. (1986). Concepts of the Inner World in George Eliot's Work, *Journal of Child Psychotherapy*, 12(2): 109–124.

7 *Joyce: Prose Poet.* Language, music and emotion

Each word has the charm of a living thing.

(Joyce)

Seamus Heaney described the great poetry of the opening chapter of *Ulysses* saying it 'amplifies and rhapsodizes the world with an unlooked-for accuracy and transport':

> It gives the spirit freedom to range in an element that is as linguistic as it is airy and watery—writing that feels so natural, spacious and unstoppably alive.
>
> (Heaney, 2002, p. 389)

Heaney points out, however, that Joyce's actual poems lack the sublime quality of the poetry of his prose. The few poems Joyce published were valued mainly for their lyrical quality—attributed to his musical upbringing. As Anthony Burgess says:

> They are charming, competent, memorable, but they would never, on their own, have made the name of the author. The 'poetic' side of Joyce (using the term in its narrowest, most orthodox sense) had to be enclosed in the irony of the great prose books for it to be effective.
>
> Joyce is most sure of himself…when he is safely encastled in a great prose structure. The poor poet, the indifferent dramatist and the casual critic take on greatness in the context of life, which is the context of the novel.
>
> (1965, pp. 75–80)

DOI: 10.4324/9781003309925-8

George Orwell was thrilled with *Ulysses:*

> Quite apart from the different styles used to represent different
> manners of thought, the observation is in places marvellous. Some
> of the passages have haunted me ever since reading them. If you
> read them aloud you will see that most of them are essentially verse.
> How extraordinarily original his mind is.
>
> (1940, p. 327)

As Kurt Vonnegut put it, 'Joyce, when he was frisky, could put together
a sentence as intricate and as glittering as a necklace for Cleopatra'.

The Music

Literary critic, Dustin Illingworth, referring to 'Araby', in *The Dubliners*, says:

> Joyce struggles to control his lyrical impulse. It registers as a kind
> of contest, a wonderful, lush distress. These sentences are absolutely
> dancing: 'Where a coachman smoothed and combed the horse and
> shook music from the buckled harness'.
>
> (twitter, 2021)

Nino Frank, on *Finnegans Wake,* wrote:

> The rhythm, the harmony, the density and consonance of the
> words were more important to him than the meaning. … Emotion
> inspired by his indestructible bond with the land that was the source
> and sustenance of his artistic personality.
>
> (1979, p. 97)

According to Litz, *Ulysses* makes use of those musical devices which are
most 'literary', counterpoint and *leitmotif*. It contains hundreds of *leitmotifs*,
repeated, amplified and transformed to create a feeling of 'musical' development. 'Joyce delights in a contrapuntal arrangement of themes: like Proust
he relies on repetition and counterpoint to advance his work' (1961, p. 65).

In the *Sirens* episode in *Ulysses*, Joyce replicates the effect of music by
using musical prose elements such as onomatopoeia, linguistic refrains
and syncopated syntax to the beautiful effect:

> Braintipped, cheek touched with flame, they listened feeling that
> flow endearing flow over skin limbs human heart soul spine.
>
> (U 352)

Here Stephen hears his father sing:

> Through the hush of air a voice sang to them, low, not rain, not leaves in murmur, like no voice of strings of reeds or what doyoucallthem dulcimers, touching their still ears with words, still hearts of their each his remembered lives.
>
> (U 353)

His love affair was with language in all its sounds, combinations and ambiguities.

Emotion

Of interest to the psychoanalyst is how Joyce managed emotion. For all the descriptions of Joyce being 'exiled in on himself' and unreachable, he was full of emotion. Writing was his way of controlling an 'over abundance' of emotion as well as a persecutory imagination. The structure of his great novels provided a 'safe castle' which the pared down poem could not. Joyce sought escape, but it would have been hard to cut off from his crippling sense of guilt and persecution and the 'nightly consternation' of his nightmares. Only epic structures could contain his struggle. Emotion, and his love affair with language, drove him. It was words, language and poetry that moved him to tears and to which he devoted his life. Burgess calls language the main character of *Ulysses*. Language would also be the star of *Finnegans Wake*. It was language that linked him forever to his brilliant conversationalist father—and to his great friend, Gogarty, with whom he spent early days reading aloud.

In his youth, Joyce's gods were Blake, Dante and Aristotle. And Homer, as he exclaimed to his friend Borach:

> The most beautiful, all-embracing theme is that of the *Odyssey*. It is greater, more human than that of *Hamlet*, *Don Quixote*, Dante, *Faust*.
>
> I find the subject of Odysseus the most human in the world literature….And the return, how profoundly human! Don't forget the trait of generosity at the interview with Ajax in the nether world, and many other beautiful touches. I am almost afraid to treat such a theme; it is overwhelming.
>
> (1979, pp. 69–70)

Jan Parandowski, a Polish novelist friend, wrote of Joyce:

> His erudition amazed me…Best of all he knew the *Odyssey* itself. He
> expounded upon many facets and features of the work, including
> the smallest details, fragments to which the glow of genius adhered,
> as a tiny rainbow does to morning dew. He derived extraordinary
> meanings from otherwise commonplace words. I listened to him
> in blissful delight.
>
> (1979, p. 157)

The themes of betrayal and guilt which run through his work come from
within. The humour and parody only add to the poignancy. Bloom's
humiliation, standing barefoot, 'apologetic toes turned in', in the *Circe*
courtroom scene, is an extended masterpiece of the tragi-comic.

> Order in court! The accused will now make a bogus statement.
> (Bloom, pleading not guilty and holding a fullblown waterlily, begins
> a long unintelligible speech. They would hear what counsel had to
> say in his stirring address to the grand jury. He was down and out
> but, though branded as a black sheep, if he might say so, he meant to
> reform, to retrieve the memory of the past in a purely sisterly way and
> return to nature as a purely domestic animal. A sevenmonths' child,
> he had been carefully brought up and nurtured by an aged bedridden
> parent. There might have been lapses of an erring father but he wanted
> to turn over a new leaf and now, when at long last in sight of the whip-
> ping post, to lead a homely life in the evening of his days, permeated
> by the affectionate surroundings of the heaving bosom of the family.)
>
> (U 587)

Full of wild energy, 'a free-wheeling circus' (Attridge), it dramatises
Bloom's fears, memories and sentimentalising as well as Stephen's sense
of guilt. To Budgen, Joyce wrote about *Circe*: 'a dreadful performance.
It gets wilder and worse and more involved but I suppose it will all
work out' (*SL*, p. 271). Written, and re-written, in a frenzy, 150 pages
with a roll call of characters from earlier chapters, Joyce called it a
'vision animated to bursting point':

> I am working like a galley slave, an ass, a brute. I cannot even sleep.
> The episode of *Circe* has changed me too into an animal. Circe her-
> self had less trouble weaving her web than I had with her episode.
>
> (Gilbert, 1957, p. 146)

But if we thought Joyce had given his all in this trial scene, there is more in *Finnegans Wake*—another court scene! For the psychoanalyst working to free narcissistic patients from the internal persecutory 'gang' (Rosenfeld, 1971), this Joycean solution, throwing himself into the madness of it, is a revelation:

> Oyeh! Oyeh! When the prisoner, soaked in methylated, appeared in dry dock, appatently ambrosiaurealised, like Kersse's Korduroy Karikature, wearing, besides stains, rents and patches, his fight shirt, straw braces, souwester and a policeman's corkscrew trowswers, all out of the true … it was attempted by the crown (P.C. Robort) to show that King, elois Crowbar, once known as Meleky, impersonating a climbing boy, rubbed some pixes of any luvial peatsmoor o'er his face, plucks and pussas, with a clanetourf as the best means of disguising himself and was to the middlewhite fair in Mudford of a Thoorsday, feishts of Peeler and Pole, under the illassumed names of Tykingfest and Rabworc picked by him and Anthony out of a tellafun book, ellegedly with a pedigree pig (unlicensed) and a hyacinth.
>
> (FW, pp. 85–86)

Joyce's cathartic and ingenious route to emotional freedom!

In the chapter of *Ulysses* before *Circe*, we are in the maternity hospital episode, *Oxen of the Sun*, where Mrs Purefoy is having difficulty giving birth to 'yet another baby'—the ninth of twelve. There is a discussion about seemingly healthy babies dying in early childhood and the state of bliss before an infant is delivered: 'Before born babe bliss had. Within womb won he worship'. Given Joyce's early agonies about his mother's constant pregnancies and, more recently, his wife Nora's miscarriage, it is as though writing the long, dense child birth chapter triggered the Lear-like four-fold 'howl' that is *Circe*. *Circe* has the feel of Lucky's mad outburst in Samuel Beckett's *Waiting for Godot*, an unstoppable flood of pent up emotion, as though Joyce no longer knows who or what he is—man, woman, dead or alive, guilty, condemned.

Joyce's description of the role of emotion in his writing is a description of how psychoanalysis works:

> Emotion has dictated the course and detail of my book, and in emotional writing one arrives at the unpredictable which can be of more value, since its sources are deeper, than the products of the intellectual method.
>
> (Norris, 2011, p. 156)

He admiringly described T. S. Eliot as 'searching for images of emotion' in his poetry.

(Power, 1974, pp. 86–87)

By giving himself clear and organised structures—and he worked immensely hard on this, witness his use of *The Odyssey* format—Joyce could immerse himself in his writing, much as the psychoanalytic patient is immersed in the transference. He observed and wrote his 'unpredictable' emotions onto the page. Describing his own development, Joyce said to Hoffmeister:

> In *Dubliners*...I wrote that the word 'paralysis' filled me with horror and fear, as though it designated something evil and sinful. I loved this word and would whisper it to myself in the evening at the open window.
>
> Each of my books is a book about Dublin—the universal city of my work. *Dubliners* was my last look at that city. Then I looked at the people around me. *Portrait* was the picture of my spiritual self. *Ulysses* transformed individual impressions and emotions to give them general significance. 'Work in Progress' has a significance completely above reality; transcending humans, things, senses and entering the realm of complete abstraction".
>
> (1979, p. 132)

Joyce could feel he had changed. To the outsider, the change in him seemed in the realm of serenity and humanity—a move from paranoid fear and reproach to a state of humility. Anthony Burgess wrote:

> No writer was more autobiographical than Joyce, but no writer ever revealed, in the telling of his story, less of himself. He keeps silent, he never judges, he never comments.
>
> No face shines through the novels of James Joyce, and this is disturbing. ...It is this preoccupation, even obsession, with the ordinary that should endear him to ordinary readers. Nobody in his books is rich or has high connections. There is no dropping of title names...and we enter no place more exalted than a pub or a public library. Ordinary people, living in an ordinary city, are invested in the riches of the ages, and these riches are enshrined in language, which is available to everybody.
>
> (1965, pp. 24–25)

As a description of Joyce as prose poet, Harry Levin said:

> More spectacularly than any of his contemporaries, Joyce embraces the extremes of richness and reality—not so much the perfect fusion of these elements as their bitter opposition. No naturalist has ventured a more exhaustive and unsparing depiction of the immediacies of daily life. No symbolist has spun more subtle and complicated cobwebs out of his own tortured entrails.
>
> (1960, p. 30)

'Ulysses' and 'The Waste Land'. Twin Revolutionary Realist Poets

Joyce's contemporary, T. S. Eliot, was one of the first to recognise the greatness of *Ulysses*:

> I hold this book to be the most important expression which the present age has found; it is a book to which we are all indebted, and from which none of us can escape….it has given me all the surprise, delight, and terror that I can require.
>
> (Eliot, 1923)

Both *The Waste Land* and *Ulysses* were published in 1922, exploding like twin modernist bombshells on literature. As Toibin describes it:

> Joyce's novel had much in common with Eliot's long poem—it dealt with the rawness of urban life using competing narrative forms, including pastiche and myth and different kinds of voices. *The Waste Land* sounded a sort of death knell for the narrative poem, just as *Ulysses* set about killing off the single-perspective, the all-knowing authorial voice.
>
> (2022)

Joyce, in admiring *The Waste Land*, saw in Eliot a fellow realist:

> Idealism is a pleasant bauble, but in these days of overwhelming reality it no longer interests us. …We regard it as a sort of theatrical drop-scene. Most lives are made up like the modern painter's themes, of jugs, and pots and plates, backstreets and blowsy living-rooms inhabited by blowsy women, and of a thousand daily

sordid incidents which seep into our minds no matter how we strive to keep them out.

(Power, 1974)

Eliot wrote *The Waste Land* in late 1921 and, in the original version, he included a drunken visit to a brothel based on Joyce's *Circe* episode. At the end, Eliot has the narrator saved from arrest by a passing Mr Donavan, just as Stephen Dedalus is saved by Corny Kelleher.

Joyce loved the jazziness of Eliot's 'Shakespeherian Rag' section (lines 128–130) and saw *The Waste Land* as, 'the expression of our time in which we are trying to lift off the accumulated weight of the ages which was stifling original thought' (Power, 1974, pp. 86–87). He knew most of Eliot's poem by heart and was not above parodying it:

Rouen is the rainiest place, getting
Inside all impermeables, wetting
Damp marrow in drenched bones. ...
     (Gross, 2010, p. 259)

There are two unforgettable recordings of Joyce's reading. He wanted the first passage from *Aeolus* to be the legacy of *Ulysses*, underscoring, according to Audrey Magee, 'his quiet but passionate desire for an independent Ireland, free of Britain and the Catholic church' (2022). The reading from *Anna Livia Plurabelle* in 1929, with his tenor voice and Irish lilt, is itself music and poetry. Edna O'Brien calls Anna his last creation: 'his farewell to words, haunting, ineffable, a mythic Eve, haloed in "the dusk of wonder"' (2017). Joyce's voice, for Seamus Heaney, was 'eddying with the vowels of all rivers...like a prosecutor's or a singer's' (1998, p. 267).

References

Borach, G. (1979). 'Conversations with James Joyce', in W. Potts, ed., *Portraits of the Artist in Exile. Recollections of James Joyce by Europeans*. Seattle: University of Washington Press, pp. 67–68.

Burgess, A. (1965). *Here Comes Everybody: An Introduction to James Joyce for the Ordinary Reader*. London: Faber and Faber.

Eliot, T. S. (1923). 'Ulysses Order and Myth', in *The Dial*, November.

Ellmann, R. ed. (1992). *Selected Letters of James Joyce*. London: Faber & Faber.

Frank, N. (1979). 'The Shadow That Had Lost Its Man', in W. Potts & N. Frank, eds., *Portraits of the Artist in Exile. Recollections of James Joyce by Europeans*. Seattle: University of Washington Press, pp. 74–105.

Gilbert, S. ed. (1957). *Selected Letters of James Joyce*, Vol. I. London: Faber & Faber.

Gross, J. ed. (2010). *The Oxford Book of Parodies*. Oxford: Oxford UP.

Heaney, S. (1998). *Opened Ground: Poems 1966–1996*. Faber & Faber.

Heaney, S. (2002). 'Joyce's Poetry', in *Finders Keepers. Selected Prose 1971–2001*. Faber, pp. 388–390.

Hoffmeister, A. (1979). 'Portrait of Joyce', in W. Potts, ed., *Portraits of the Artist in Exile. Recollections of James Joyce by Europeans*. Seattle: University of Washington Press, pp. 119–136.

Joyce, J. (1961). *Ulysses*. New York: Random House.

Litz, A. W. (1961). *The Art of James Joyce: Method and Design in Ulysses* and *Finnegans Wake*. Oxford: Oxford University Press.

Magee, A. (2022). 'Unbind the tongue': Joyce and the Irish language, in the Centenary Year of Ulysses, *Times Literary Supplement*, February.

Norris, M. (2011). 'Finnegans Wake', in *Cambridge Companion to James Joyce*, D. Attridge, ed. Cambridge: Cambridge University Press, pp. 149–171.

O'Brien, E. (2017). How James Joyce's Anna Livia Plurabelle Shook the Literary World, *The Guardian,* January.

Orwell, G. (1940). *Inside the Whale and Other Essays*. London: Gollanz.

Parandowski, J. (1979). 'Meeting with Joyce', in W. Potts, ed., *Portraits of the Artist in Exile. Recollections of James Joyce by Europeans*. Seattle: University of Washington Press, pp. 153–162.

Power, A. (1974). *Conversations with James Joyce,* ed. C. Hart. New York: Columbia UP.

Rosenfeld, H. (1971). A Clinical Approach to the Psychoanalytic Theory of the Life and Death Instincts: An Investigation into the Aggressive Aspects of Narcissism, *International Journal of Psychoanalysis*, 52: 169–178.

Toibin, C. (2022). Ulysses at 100. The Birth of the Modern. *Financial Times.*

8 *Gogarty: The Lost Brother.* James Joyce, 'Buck Mulligan' and the Martello Tower

> The Martello Tower pages are full of beauty, a cruel,
>   playful mind like a great, soft tiger cat.
>
> W. B. Yeats (Gogarty, p. 26)

This chapter is about the intense love/hate brotherly relationship between James Joyce and Oliver St John Gogarty, immortalised at the beginning of *Ulysses*. The attachment and rivalry between them, between the usurper and the legitimate one, mirrors the tragedy of the replacement child. While Joyce spent his life in exile, dreaming of and writing about Dublin, the immensely popular and brilliant Gogarty, hailed by his close friend, W. B. Yeats, as 'one of the great lyric poets of the age', remained at the centre of life in Dublin like the favoured and legitimate son that Joyce could never be.

The beginning of *Ulysses*, one of the most memorable openings in a novel, places a formidable Buck Mulligan and a struggling Stephen Dedalus centre stage. Capturing the early morning, ensconced in their tower, with views across to the 'awaking mountains', it introduces Stephen's impossible attraction to Mulligan and his own 'poor dogsbody' recalcitrance.

Stately, plump Buck Mulligan came from the stair head, bearing a bowl of lather on which a mirror and a razor lay crossed. A yellow dressing gown, ungirdled, was sustained gently behind him on the mild morning air. He held the bowl aloft and intoned:
Introibo ad altare Dei.
Halted, he peered down the dark winding stairs and called out coarsely:
Come up, Kinch! Come up, you fearful jesuit!

DOI: 10.4324/9781003309925-9

Solemnly he came forward and mounted the round gun rest. He faced about and blessed gravely thrice the tower, the surrounding land and the awaking mountains. Then, catching sight of Stephen Dedalus, he bent towards him and made rapid crosses in the air, gurgling in his throat and shaking his head. Stephen Dedalus, displeased and sleepy, leaned his arms on the top of the staircase and looked coldly at the shaking gurgling face that blessed him, equine in its length, and at the light untonsured hair, grained and hued like pale oak.

Published in 1922, the setting is the Martello Tower in Dublin's Sandymount, above the famous 'Forty Foot' swimming area. The scene is based on real life from 1904 when Joyce rented the tower with Gogarty, 'Buck Mulligan'. Two years older than Joyce, Gogarty was an exciting, larger than life character, in many ways the opposite of Joyce, but a poet with an astonishing memory to rival Joyce's and very drawn to his intellect.

They met in 1901 when Gogarty was studying medicine at Trinity College and Joyce was at University College. They became inseparable:

Only a few months after meeting, Joyce and Gogarty had already become a familiar pair in the city streets. For a year or so they were seldom out of each other's company—striding along arm in arm, a handsome pair of mockers whispering irreverences in each other's ears. Whenever a remark of Gogarty's particularly pleased Joyce, he would stop deliberately, throw back his head, and guffaw loudly.

(O'Connor, 2000, p. 67)

That the friendship was intense can be seen in the many letters from Gogarty when he was in Oxford for two terms in 1904. Often helping him out financially, Gogarty pressed Joyce to visit him: 'Be Jaysus Joyce. You must come over here. ...I shall send you travelling expenses (I couldn't trust you with more.) ...I want to get dhrunk, dhrunk' (O'Connor, 2000, p. 73).

In Dublin, they enjoyed the nightlife together frequenting pubs and brothels and they spent their days sharing a love of literature and the classics. As Gogarty described it:

We walked in that garden for many eager days. We talked of the poets. In my garden the apple trees were in bloom, and there is bloom in the first of the lyrics he reluctantly showed me— Tennysonian, exquisite things:

My love is in a light attire
Among the apple trees
Where the young winds do most desire
To run in companies.
  (1990, p. 22)

In *Ulysses*, Joyce alludes to their attachment as being a 'love that dare not speak its name' (Wilde) and portrays Gogarty as the only person who will stand up to him and challenge him, as a father might.

Jennifer Levine points out the richness with which Joyce portrays Buck Mulligan at the beginning of *Ulysses*. He is full of life and colour in his 'yellow dressinggown, ungirdled...sustained gently behind him on the mild morning air':

> In 'Telemachus' every gesture and utterance of Mulligan's is empha-
> sized with an adjective, or an adverb, or a richly descriptive verb.
> Stephen, in contrast, 'displeased and sleepy', looks 'coldly' at him,
> merely steps up, follows him 'wearily, and asks 'quietly'. Mulligan
> in the first two pages, 'intones', calls out 'coarsely', gurgles 'in his
> throat', 'adds 'in a preacher's tone', gives a 'long slow whistle', and
> laughs 'with delight....Stephen is silent for almost fifty lines until
> he finally 'says': first 'quietly', then 'with energy and growing fear'.
>   (2004, p. 126)

Levine is reminded of the scene in Hamlet where Claudius is 'hogging the show', wearing brilliant royal robes:

> [He] stands centre stage, and holds the full attention of his court
> while he speaks, and speaks and speaks. Hamlet, meanwhile,
> dressed all in black, stands to the side. And says very little that is
> not private and for his ears only.
>   (Ibid, p. 126)

Gogarty's importance to Joyce is strangely minimised in the scholarly literature even though his presence as Buck Mulligan at the start of *Ulysses* is unforgettable. Perhaps this is because Joyce was mostly silent about him after he left Dublin, the same way he was silent about his mother after her early death.

Gogarty's biographer, Ulick O'Connor, (another colourful Dublin figure), portrays him as a totally fascinating character. He was from a wealthy Dublin family, a lifelong friend of W. B. Yeats, a fellow Senator, and famous for his wit, his limericks and his bravery. O'Connor's biography was published in 1964 (the director John Ford praised it as the only book he stayed up all night to read), but Joyce's biographer, Richard Ellman, makes no reference to it.

After finishing at University College in 1903, Joyce went to Paris to try (like Gogarty) for a medical degree but soon returned to Dublin to spend four months with his dying mother. This was an immensely difficult time for Joyce, resurrecting painful childhood separations from her, and Gogarty describes Joyce as 'undergoing an inward change. Revolt and scorn were increasing' (1990, p. 26). They initially wanted to rent the Martello Tower together for a year so that Joyce could concentrate on writing his book. Gogarty had dreams of the Martello Tower as a new *omphalos*, a centre of new creativity. In a seashore setting worthy of Hamlet's Elsinore, it was away from the town and with wonderful views. Gogarty describes their arrival:

> We saw a little door, and upon opening it, discovered a flight of steps in the thickness of the wall. Full of adventure, we ascended. What a pleasant discovery! There was a platform of granite and a circular raised wall from which you could see over the battlements head high. There was the Hill of Howth that formed the northern arm of Dublin Bay lying purple in the light. Dublin lay to the west, a dull ruby under a canopy of smoke. The sight fascinated Joyce. For a long time he gazed at his native town, 'The Seventh City of Christendom'.... 'This will do for a table,' Joyce said, pointing to the gun emplacement, 'and we can sit in the step and move around with the sun. We can do as much sunbathing as we wish. Nobody can see us here. We can see everyone when we look over the parapet. We overlooked everything from our seventy-foot eminence. When we ascended to the living room, very formally Joyce 'took possession' by laying his roll of poems on the shelf.
>
> (1990, p. 23)

Gogarty describes them living 'in privacy and profanity': 'I could take it easy on the roof, for I shunned work; Joyce could remain downstairs forever reading and re-reading his 'Contra Gentiles, an early essay against everybody" (Ibid, p.27). This conveys his view of Joyce as changed and rejecting—'the great denier'. Gogarty, a strong athlete, loved the 40-foot bathing-pool below the Tower, swimming in the sunset 'when the water becomes soft and crimson-flecked'. Joyce, a 'splashy swimmer but fast' would only sometimes join him (O'Connor, 2000, p. 81).

Tragically, things fell apart between them. Joyce, always emotionally fragile, was especially so after his mother's death. Throughout his life, his writing held him together. The image of him in the tower, in a world of his own, has a womb-like quality. Although Gogarty respected Joyce's need to write, he also longed for his company. He was a compulsive talker—famous for holding forth for hours at a time. (One look at his three-volume autobiography confirms that image.)

About Gogarty's conversational style, George Moore wrote:

> His power of perceiving distant analogies, piling imagination upon imagination, spinning his speech out as a butterfly spins from a chrysalis...how he became restless if kept out of the conversation too long, like an athlete waiting to get into the arena.
>
> (O'Connor, 2000, p. 51)

Gogarty described an increasing seriousness in Joyce's demeanour, his silences, and being unable to rally him from 'being sullen in the sweet air': *'Why do I put up with him at all? It must be the attraction of opposites that holds us together'*.

Joyce famously and abruptly left the tower after only a week when Gogarty brought another friend to stay—the Oxbridge Englishman, Haines. The appearance of usurpers and a sense of betrayal, powerful themes throughout Joyce's writing, led things to implode in the Tower. In *Ulysses,* Stephen's last word as he leaves is, 'Usurper!' This is the word Joyce's father used about Joyce 'usurping the cot of his dead brother'. Joyce didn't begin writing *Ulysses* for another ten years, but the writing is raw and intense, as though Joyce's feelings about that time were still very much alive.

Curiously there is no hint of the fact that Joyce had met Nora just three months before he moved into the Tower. His letters to her at this time show him obsessed with her. It is not clear how much Gogarty knew about this, but when Joyce left Ireland Gogarty was derogatory, referring to Nora as a 'slavey'. There is also nothing in *Ulysses* alluding to Nora's existence—Stephen goes with prostitutes but has no love interest. Of his family, his father, Simon Dedalus, appears, and his dead mother haunts him; one sister appears poignantly briefly but Stephen is portrayed as lost and alone in an aimless existence after his mother's death.

Joyce scholars had a heated debate about who was the usurper at the Martello Tower, who paid the rent, who rejected whom. The extraordinary back and forth on this issue seemed to reflect the tragic inner debate of the replacement child who is full of confusion, guilt and resentment, not knowing who to blame for not being the 'legiti-mate' one. Joyce's father viewed him as the usurper, while Joyce viewed mother's other babies as usurpers (Jackson and Costello, 1997, p. 112).

I have described Joyce's various ways of holding together in the face of emotional dissolution all his life, being absorbed in his writing as an obvious one. Entering inside the object (by intrusive identification) is also a way the uncontained child tries to keep control. Joyce liked to get right inside everywhere and while this offers the illusion of control, it also draws one into an enclosed claustrum-like world, cut off from the real world. The Martello Tower may have been away from the centre of Dublin, and with wonderful seascape views, but Joyce seemed to feel crowded in and quickly claustrophobic. Like a psychoanalyst, Gogarty tries to lift him back 'into the sweet air' but he fails, saying about Joyce: 'A desert was revealed which I did not think existed amid the seeming luxuriance of his soul' (O'Connor, 2000, p. 82).

The fact that Joyce immortalised Gogarty in *Ulysses* conveyed how drawn he was to him. Gogarty claimed to be hurt by the book: 'That bloody Joyce whom I kept in my youth has written a book you can read on all the lavatory walls of Dublin' (1990, 61). But Joyce casts himself as the scornful, difficult one and Gogarty seems to have been hurt more by the loss of their friendship. Things are lively between them in the literary Episode 9 of *Ulysses*—'Scylla and Charybdis' being an apt description of the two of them, now separated by the Atlantic rather than Homer's Straits of Messina. When Mulligan is asked about Shakespeare, he responds:

> – Shakespeare? he said. I seem to know the name.
> A flying sunny smile rayed in his loose features.
> – To be sure, he said, remembering brightly. The chap that writes like Synge.

In their last brief meeting, Gogarty quipped to Joyce affectionately: 'I don't care a damn what you say of me so long as it is literature'.

As well as the strong relationship between Joyce and Nora, Joyce developed close male friendships in Europe. One friend, Louis Gillet, wrote that for Joyce love appeared to be an exclusively male function, 'a virile abstract affection…a current going from man to man' (1979, p. 190). Heffner, looking at the ambiguity of gender and sexuality in *Ulysses,* uses the sharing of shoes as an example of intimacy between Gogarty and Joyce and points out that Joyce is comparing Mulligan to Cranly, Stephen's 'staunch friend' and 'brother soul' from *Portrait of the Artist as a Young Man* (2017, p. 21). Joyce writes:

> His gaze brooded on his broadtoed boots, a buck's castofs, nebenein-
> ander. He counted the creases of rucked leather wherein another's

foot has nested warm. The foot that beat the ground in tripudium, foot I dislove. But you were delighted when Esther Osvalt's shoe went on you: girl I knew in Paris. Tiens, quel petit pied! Staunch friend, a brother soul: Wilde's love that dare not speak its name. His arm: Cranly's arm. He now will leave me. And the blame? As I am. As I am. All or not at all.

(U, p. 62)

There were attempts to resume the friendship with Gogarty when Joyce was living in Trieste. A request from Joyce in 1906 that Gogarty might visit him drew an enthusiastic reply. Expressing, poetically, his old love for Joyce, he said he missed in the letter 'the touch of a vanished hand and the sound of a voice that is still'. It is not known if Gogarty did visit but in 1907 they were corresponding in their old familiar terms with Gogarty keen to have Joyce visit him in Vienna. He also suggested that he would pay for a summer tour of the Mediterranean by steamer on which they would write verses together in the old familiar fashion while he would undertake to pay the fares. Joyce's brother, Stanislaus, envious of their friendship discouraged this. He saw Gogarty as a tempting Joyce away from his writing.

When Nora saw in the newspaper that Gogarty had married, Joyce responded plaintively, 'I suppose he wouldn't dare present me to his wife' (Maddox, 1988, p. 103). In fact, Gogarty did invite him to visit them, but Joyce refused.

Gogarty remained a prominent figure in Dublin life and it would have been easy for Joyce to keep track of him. He became an eminent eye, ear, nose and throat surgeon as well as a senator and was a close friend of Yeats. He was fearless in his exploits. Once when kidnapped by IRA militants, he escaped by leaping into the River Liffey, promising he would donate two swans if he survived, which he did. He had three children, drove around in a Rolls Royce, was brilliant at limericks and would recite long poems from memory. Gogarty was at the centre of Dublin where Joyce could never be—except by writing *Ulysses* and *Finnegans Wake*.

Gogarty appears in Joyce's exuberant trial scenes, as here in *Finnegans Wake*:

Remarkable evidence was given, anon, by an eye, ear, nose and throat witness, whom Wesleyan chapelgoers suspected of being a plain clothes priest W.P., situate at Nullnull, Medical Square, who, upon letting down his rice and peacegreen coverdisk and having been sullenly cautioned against yawning while being grilled, smiled (he had had a onebumper at parting from Mrs Molroe in the morning) and stated to his eliciter under his morse mustaccents (gobbless!) that he slept with a bonafides and that he would be there to remember the filth of November....

both changelings, unlucalised, of no address and in noncommunicables, between him and whom, ever since wallops before the Mise of Lewes, bad blood existed on the ground of the boer's trespass on the bull or because he firstparted his polarbeeber hair in twoways, or because they were creepfoxed andt grousuppers over a nippy in a noveletta, or because they could not say meace, (mute and daft) meathe.

(FW, p. 86)

As I describe in Chapter 9, while Joyce was writing *Ulysses*, Gogarty, for all his enjoyment of the high life, was devoted to giving free medical treatment to the Dublin poor, speaking out about the 'inferno' tenement conditions. As Grennan describes:

Surgeon to the rich, he administered gratis to the poor. Living a life of personal and professional privilege, he was a vocal advocate of improved social conditions for the scandalously housed poor of Dublin. Comic blasphemer, irreverent skeptic, praised as Dublin's 'arch-mocker and wit', he was the generous friend of priests and nuns.

(2007, *Irish Times*)

In 1917, he wrote the first 'slum' play exposing the conditions. Joyce would have been well aware of this.

Poignantly, the two books on Joyce's desk when he died were *I Follow St Patrick,* by Gogarty, and a Greek dictionary, presumably to look up words used by Gogarty. After Joyce died, Gogarty said: 'To this day I am sorry for that thoughtless horseplay on such a hypersensitive and difficult friend' (1990, p. 31).

References

Gillet, L. (1979). 'The Living Joyce', in W. Potts, ed., *Portraits of the Artist in Exile. Recollections of James Joyce by Europeans.* Seattle: University of Washington Press, pp. 170–204.

Gogarty, O. St. J. (1990). 'James Joyce: A Portrait of the Artist', in E. H. Mikhail, ed., *James Joyce. Interviews and Recollections.* The Macmillan Press, London, pp. 21–32.

Grennan, E. (2007). 'The Clown Prince of the Literary Revival', *Irish Times*, November 3.

Heffner, S. (2017). *Blurring the Lines: The Ambiguity of Gender and Sexuality in Ulysses*. San Antonio, TX: Trinity University.

Jackson, J. W., & Costello, P. (1997). *John Stanislaus Joyce: The Voluminous Life and Genius of James Joyce's Father*. London: Fourth Estate.

Levine, J. (2004). 'Ulysses', in D. Attridge, ed., *The Cambridge Companion to James Joyce*. Cambridge: Cambridge UP, pp. 122–148.

Maddox, B. (1988). *Nora: A Biography of Nora Joyce*. Greenwich, CT: Fawcett Books.

O'Connor, U. (2000). *Oliver St John Gogarty. A Poet and His Times*. Dublin: O'Brien Press.

9   *The Sorrow of Ulysses*
'Deathflower of the potato
blight on her breast'

In *Ulysses,* we have the story of a couple, Molly and Bloom, their lives shattered by the loss of their baby son, and the wandering Stephen Dedalus haunted by his mother's death, trying to escape history and the paralysis around him. Joyce has written an epic of devastating grief—his own and Ireland's.

Joyce was only one generation away from the Great Famine. As described by Colm Toibin:

> Around a million people died of disease, hunger and fever in the years between 1846 and 1849. The West of Ireland suffered most and there are people there today who claim to be haunted still by the silences and absences and emptiness that the Famine left. John Mitchel claimed the Famine was genocide: 'It could have been prevented by the British…Ireland was exporting to England food to the value of £15 million, and had on her own soil…good and ample provision for double her own population'. On some 'coffin ships', the death rate was more than 50 per cent.
>
> (2001, p. 9)

Thousands of tenants were evicted and left in mud huts to die. In 1847, almost 300,000 people arrived in Liverpool from Ireland. Of these, 116,000 were 'half naked and starving'. A great silence befell Ireland— the singing stopped, the Irish language was lost, people were speechless from the trauma.

Joyce's close friend, the playwright J. M. Synge, whose grandfather died of famine fever, wrote the first 'famine' play, *Playboy of the Western World*. The Famine is not named but the images are unmistakable: a lone figure lying in a ditch in the Irish countryside, moaning to the point of being subhuman; the wail of the 'keener'—Pegeen putting her shawl over her head and breaking into 'wild lamentations'.

DOI: 10.4324/9781003309925-10

Ulysses was banned and damned for 'obscenity', but the true obscenity was the oppression and suffering endured by the Irish. In his public lectures in Trieste, Joyce was openly critical:

> The English now laugh at the Irish for being Catholic, poor and ignorant...Ireland is poor because English laws destroyed the industries of the country, notably the woollen one; because in the years in which the potato crop failed, the negligence of the English government left the flower of the people to die in hunger.
>
> (1907, p. 119)

In *Ulysses* and *Finnegans Wake*, the Famine is an underlying presence. Kevin Whelan says, 'Beneath its calm surface, *Ulysses* is pervasively disturbed by the presence of the Famine. The post-Famine condition of Ireland is the unnamed horror at the heart of Joyce's Irish darkness' (2012, *Irish Times*).

The image of women mourning, wailing and 'keening', so linked with the Famine, appears in *Ulysses* as an 'Old Gummy Granny' 'rocking to and fro...keen[ing] with banshee woe'. *Finnegans Wake* has a mock wake in its first few pages including a 'duodisimally profusive plethora of ululation...kankan keening'. Leopold Bloom is obsessed with food and carries with him a potato. In *Proteus,* Joyce writes:

> Famine, plague and slaughters. Their blood is in me, their lusts my waves. I moved among them on the frozen Liffey, that I, a changeling, among the spluttering resin fires. I spoke to no-one: none to me.
>
> (U, p. 56)

This powerful quote is also striking for Stephen identifying as a 'changeling'—the image of a replacement child.

Other images of the Famine appear in the episode of *Lestrygonians* where famished skeletons contrast with plentiful food. Bloom is ready for lunch but sees Stephen's 'malnourished' sister, Dilly. In *Cyclops*, Joyce rails about the Famine:

> We'll put force against force, says the citizen. We have our greater Ireland beyond the sea. They were driven out of house and home in the black 47. Their mudcabins and their shielings by the roadside were laid low by the batteringram and the *Times* rubbed its hands and told the whitelivered Saxons there would soon be as few Irish in Ireland as redskins in America. Even the Grand Turk sent us his piastres. But the Sassenach tried to starve the nation at home while

the land was full of crops that the British hyenas bought and sold in Rio de Janeiro. Ay, they drove out the peasants in hordes. Twenty thousand of them died in the coffinships. But those that came to the land of the free remember the land of bondage. And they will come again and with a vengeance, no cravens, the sons of Granuaile, the champions of Kathleen ni Houlihan.

(U, pp. 427–428)

Bonnie Roos interprets *Ulysses* as a metaphor for the oppression and suffering during the Famine, especially of Irish women:

There is no room for love in famine: mothers sometimes stole food from their children, or murdered them in an attempt to end their suffering; prostitution became a way for a woman to feed herself and, in some cases, her husband or family....Angered by his mother's voicelessness, which has become his own, Stephen, emulating Synge's Playboy Christy, kills his mother's ghost. He still remains unawakened from the nightmare of history, and his/ story.

(2005, p. 190)

Conditions for the poor in Dublin in Joyce's time were appalling. While Joyce was writing *Ulysses* in Trieste, his friend Gogarty was a surgeon treating poor families in Dublin and writing a play, *Blight*, exposing the conditions of 'the most fearful slums in Europe'. The tenement houses were compared to Dante's *Inferno* with 'over a hundred tenants and only one toilet'. Gogarty's play was the first *slum* play, ahead of those by Synge and O'Casey. It opened at the Abbey Theatre in December 1917, caused a sensation, and was taken off after ten days because of its impact (O'Connor, 2000, pp. 150–156).

Fintan O'Toole describes the child abuse at every level of the state and educational system in Ireland, punishment of women as sexual beings, bans against birth control and homosexuality, rampant sexual abuse, corporal punishment in the schools, institutions for unmarried mothers. The Artane schools for orphaned boys were notorious and greatly feared for the oppression and terrors: 'The violence within them radiated a dark energy of horror, a constant, invisible pulse of anxiety'. O'Toole was startled to find Artane in *Ulysses* 'as a sinister shadow, already imprinted on the imaginary life of the city':

Leopold Bloom goes to the funeral of Paddy Dignam and the men discuss the fate of his young son: 'Martin is trying to get the youngster into Artane'. Later on in the night-town dream world, 'Artane orphans, joining hands, caper round' Bloom. The place flits in and out of consciousness, never quite coming into focus but always there as a portent, a sequel, the unseen fate that awaits the innocent boy. …It wasn't literary modernism. It was social realism.

(2021, p. 517)

Colm Toibin adds:

Since corporal punishment in schools continued until as recently as the early 80s, anyone who had the misfortune to be educated by priests or Christian Brothers (or indeed nuns) would have fully recognised the scene where Stephen is unfairly punished. It happened to us all.

(*Guardian*, 2016)

By going into exile, Joyce was following the thousands forced to flee during the Famine. It is hard to imagine his turmoil leaving his family and grieving for his mother. He was filled with anger at Ireland which he blamed for his mother's death and the pain of his father's decline. He had to contend, too, with rejection by publishers. His furious broadside, *Gas from a Burner* (1912), was written in response to an Irish printer reneging on a contract, and destroying the proofs of *Dubliners*. It parodies the publisher and includes these lines:

But I owe a duty to Ireland:
I held her honour in my hand,
This lovely land that always sent
Her writers and artists to banishment
O Ireland my first and only love
Where Christ and Caesar are hand and glove!
I wish you could see what tears I weep
When I think of the emigrant train and ship.
That's why I publish far and wide
My quite illegible railway guide,
In the porch of my printing institute
The poor and deserving prostitute
Plays every night at catch-as-catch-can
With her tight-breeched British artilleryman
And the foreigner learns the gift of the gab
From the drunken draggletail Dublin drab.

Franco Bruni describes Joyce in Trieste:

> His spirit, particularly when he was depressed, would always return to Ireland. And if you were to ask him then what was on his mind, you would have heard a man discuss the torment of his country, showering it with mockery, while drowning his grimaces in a flow of unrestrainable tears.
>
> (1979, p. 41)

Ulysses seems a waystation between *Dubliners* and *Finnegans Wake* as Joyce adjusts to exile and reflects on his homeland. His well of anger produces parody and mockery, while his grief and artistic sensibility become astonishing poetry. Despite his anger, as John Berger pointed out, Joyce wrote 'with equanimity and without hate'. Limiting *Ulysses* to a single day in Dublin allows Joyce to portray the inner world of the Dublin he knew, interweaving the individual suffering and national trauma.

Colum McCann, in GQ, described *Ulysses* as the most complete literary compendium of human experience. 'Every time I read it, it leaves me alert and raw'. George Orwell, admiring Joyce's realism, wrote:

> Joyce is attempting to select and represent events and thoughts as they occur in life and not as they occur in fiction. The effect is to break down, at any rate momentarily, the solitude in which the human being lives. When you read certain passages you feel that Joyce's mind and your mind are one, that he knows all about you though he has never heard your name, that there exists some world outside time and space in which you and he are together.
>
> (1940, p. 327)

Declan Kiberd says, 'parody is the act of a trapped mind which, realizing that it cannot create anew, takes its revenge by defacing the masterpieces of the past' (1992, p. xlviii). It is impressive to see the way Joyce worked through the sense of revenge and betrayal that consumed him early on. The parody in *Finnegans Wake* has new compassion and is qualitatively different from that in *Ulysses*—gone is the revenge. It compares, for example, with that of Shakespeare and Samuel Beckett. As Michael and Margaret Rustin describe, Beckett's humour conveys not only the humanity of his characters but also 'the pity and understanding of the characters for each other' (2000, p. 171). Leopold Bloom in *Ulysses* feels a kind of pity for others, but remains isolated and bereft of human intercourse. In Shakespeare, revenge and betrayal give way to 'let it be' (Scene 5:2) in *Hamlet,* reconciliation in *The Winter's Tale* and the relinquishing of omnipotence in *The Tempest.*

Joyce did not have the experience of psychoanalysis, but his emotional growth can surely be attributed to his passionate immersion in great literature. Joyce was famed for his ability to recite long passages of poetry, especially Dante, as well as the Bible. Franco Bruni felt that as a genius Joyce 'was sovereign': 'He understood Dante and could explicate him with the insight of a genius…I saw him many times with tears in his eyes after such a reading' (1979, p. 44). Robert McAlmon, describing their late evenings in Paris, recalled: 'Inevitably there came a time when drink so moved his spirit that he began quoting from his own work or reciting long passages of Dante in rolling sonorous Italian, as though saying mass' (1990, p. 105).

David Black writes about the 'deep psychological truthfulness with which Dante deals with the painful personal crisis that underlies the poem'. It is a truthfulness and intellectual struggle with which Joyce would have identified. He may also have appreciated Black's 'Two Suns' analysis of the way Dante was drawn to both the *classical* and *Christian* traditions (Black, 2017, p. 2). Joyce himself spoke of the contrast between classical literature and modern:

> To my mind [the classical style] is a form of writing which contains little or no mystery, and since we are surrounded by mystery it has always seemed to me inadequate. …It is an intellectual approach which no longer satisfies the modern mind, which is interested above all in subtleties, equivocations and the subterranean complexities which dominate the average man and compose his life. …We are now anxious to explore the hidden world, those undercurrents which flow beneath the apparently firm surface. …Our object is to create a new fusion between the exterior world and our contemporary selves, and also to enlarge our vocabulary of the subconscious as Proust has done…. Sensation is our object, heightened even to the point of hallucination.
>
> Eliot has a mind which can appreciate and express both and by placing one in contrast to the other he has obtained striking effects.
>
> (Power, 1999, p. 1384)

After the sorrow and paralysis of *Ulysses, Finnegans Wake* is indeed filled with new life, 'sensation' and 'subterranean complexities'. Anna Livia Plurabelle, the involved wife and mother in *Finnegans Wake,* is a different person from the bereft and lonely Molly of *Ulysses.* The washerwomen support each other and the rivalrous twin brothers, Shem and Shaun (Joyce and the lost brother?), are united:

> We're as thick and thin now as two tubular jawballs. I hate him about his patent henesy, pfasfh it, yet am I amorist. I love him. I love his old portugal's nose.

> (FW 463)

Ulysses Publication Day—*Joyce's Birthday* 2/2/1922

The excitement on the day of the delivery of the newly published *Ulysses* had Joyce in a state of 'energetic prostration'. Two copies were sent from the printers in Dijon on the Dijon-Paris express to arrive at 7 a.m. Sylvia Beach picked them up and took a ten-minute taxi ride to Joyce giving him one copy and taking the other for display in her shop. 'Everyone crowded in from 9 o'clock until closing time to see it' (*JJ*, p. 524).

> Joyce and friends dined in the Italian restaurant, *Ferrari's*. Joyce sat at the head of the table, sideways, his legs crossed…He wore a new ring, a reward he had promised himself years before. He seemed already melancholy, sighing now and then as he ordered dinner and ate nothing. There was a toast to the book and its author which left Joyce deeply moved.

> (*Ibid*)

References

Black, D. (2017). Dante's 'Two Suns': Reflections on the Psychological Sources of the Divine Comedy, *The International Journal of Psychoanalysis*, 98(6): 1699–1717.

Bruni, F. (1979). 'Recollections of Joyce', in W. Potts, ed., *Portraits of the Artist in Exile. Recollections of James Joyce by Europeans*. Seattle: University of Washington Press, pp. 39–46.

Joyce, J. (1907). 'Ireland: Island of Saints and Sages', in *Occasional, Critical, and Political Writing*, 2000/2008. Oxford: Oxford World Classics, pp. 108–126.

Kiberd, D. (1992). Introduction: James Joyce, *Ulysses, Annotated Student Edition*. London: Penguin, pp. ix–lxxx.

McAlmon, R. (1990). 'With James Joyce', in E. H. Mikhail, ed., *James Joyce: Interviews & Recollections*. London: Macmillan Press, p. 103.

O'Connor, U. (2000). *Oliver St John Gogarty. A Poet and His Times*. Dublin: O'Brien Press.

Orwell, G. (1940). *Inside the Whale and Other Essays*. London: Gollanz.

O'Toole, F. (2021). *We Don't Know Ourselves, A Personal History of Ireland since 1958*, Head of Zeus.

Power, A. (1999). *Conversations with Joyce*. Dublin: The Lilliput Press. [Kindle Edition].

Roos, B. (2005). 'The Joyce of Eating: Feast, Famine and the Humble Potato in *Ulysses*', in G. Cusack & S. Goss, eds., *Hungry Words. Images of Famine in the Irish Canon, (2006)*. Dublin: Irish Academic Press, pp. 159–196.

Rustin, M. (2000). 'Beckett: Dramas of Psychic Catastrophe', in M. Cohen & A. Hahn, eds., *Exploring the Work of Donald Meltzer: A Festschrift*. Karnac Books, pp. 152–172.

Toibin, C. (2016). James Joyce's Portrait of the Artist, 100 years on, *Guardian*, December.

Toibin, C., & Ferriter, D. (2001). *The Irish Famine. A Documentary*. New York: St Martin's Press.

Whelan, K. (2012). The Long Shadow of the Great Hunger, *Irish Times*, September 1, 2012.

10 Medievalism to Modernity. His Own *Book of Kells*

If I had lived in the 15th Century I should have been more appreciated.

[Joyce]

Finnegans Wake is described as Joyce's own *Book of Kells*, the 7th century illuminated Latin copy of the Four Gospels—the most beautiful Irish book in existence (Figure 10.1). 'Our book of kills', Joyce called it. He kept a reproduction of this ancient testament with him wherever he lived. 'You can compare much of my work to the intricate designs of the illuminations' he said, 'and I have poured over its workmanship for hours at a time' (*JJ*, p. 545). Colm Toibin wrote:

> It is easy to see from these illustrations why Joyce loved the book so much. There is a sense of the ingenious mind at work in every page. Just as we can imagine Joyce's glittering talent as he created the patterns and tones of *Ulysses* and the word puzzles of *Finnegans Wake*, some pages of *The Book of Kells* can be best viewed as work in progress, the monks filling in gaps with elaborate coloured puzzles, snaking and looping lines, knots and interlacings. They used decoration for its own sake and colour for the delight it offered; they brought calligraphy to a fine and playful art.
>
> (2012)

To his friend, Arthur Power, Joyce noted:

> In all the places I have been to, Rome, Zurich, Trieste, I have taken it about with me. It is the most purely Irish thing we have,

DOI: 10.4324/9781003309925-11

and some of the big initial letters which swing right across the page
have the essential quality of a chapter of Ulysses.

(Ibid, 2012)

The image of Joyce 'pouring over it for hours' gives a sense of the
in-depth study Joyce was famous for. Colm Toibin points out that, as
well as their Biblical learning and artistic talent, the monks 'were having

Figure 10.1 Chi Rho, *Book of Kells*

the time of their lives', displaying great wit in their illustrations—something Joyce would have enjoyed (*Ibid*, 2012).

One wonders how much he and fellow Irishmen, Samuel Beckett, admired the *Book of Kells* together. Beckett himself was known for detailed study of great paintings, often having them in mind when staging his plays. 'He writes his paintings!' said his favourite actress, Billie Whitelaw.

Describing himself as writing in a medieval tradition, Joyce said: 'The Irish are still a medieval people and Dublin a medieval city with those medieval taverns in which the sacred and the obscene rub shoulders'. Peter Chrisp describes Joyce as 'in a medieval frame of mind' when he began writing *Finnegans Wake,* and points out that the early sketches were based on Irish medieval myths and history—King Roderick O'Conor, St Patrick and the Druid, Tristan and Isolde, The Annals of the Four Masters and St Kevin. Most medieval in style is the St Kevin piece, which is structured according to ecclesiastical and angelical hierarchies, liturgical colours, canonical hours, gifts of the Holy Spirit and the seven sacraments. 'Dante would have felt at home with this way of writing a book' (Chrisp, 2013).

Joyce also spent hours looking at the 1914 Edward Sullivan text about the manuscript which describes, 'the creeping undulations of serpentine forms, that writhe in artistic profusion throughout the mazes of its decoration' (Chrisp, p. 1). In *Finnegans Wake,* alluding to the recovery of the *Book of Kells* from under a sod after its theft in 1007, Joyce has the famous letter written by Anna Livia discovered in a rubbish heap by a neighbour's hen:

> the sudden spluttered petulance of some capitalized mIddle; a word as cunningly hidden in its maze of confused drapery as a field mouse in a nest of coloured ribbons.
>
> (FW, p. 120)

The way Joyce worked was worthy of a medieval monk as described by Harry Levin:

> Just as its richly elaborated illustrations obscure the letters of the Book of Kells, so the strange conglomerated words of Joyce's invention obscure the simple stories of the *Wake* ... No naturalist has ventured a more exhaustive and unsparing depiction of the immediacies of daily life. No symbolist has spun more subtle and complicated cobwebs out of his own tortured entrails.
>
> (1960, p. 18)

From the Medieval to the Modern

Umberto Eco described *Finnegans Wake* as 'a node where the Middle Ages and the avant-garde meet'. Joyce's modernism focuses on life's specifics in all its permutations. His 'exhaustive and unsparing depiction of the immediacies of daily life', as Levin puts it, gives a picture of both the medieval quality of Joyce's work and the realism which Joyce identifies as his modernism. As he described to Power:

> In realism you get down to facts on which the world is based; that sudden reality which smashes romanticism into a pulp. …Nature is quite unromantic. It is we who put romance into her, which is a false attitude, an egotism, absurd like all egotism. In *Ulysses* I tried to keep close to fact.
>
> (Power, 1999)

Joyce described writing *Ulysses* 'from eighteen different points of view and in as many styles…all apparently unknown or undiscovered by my fellow tradesmen' (Butler, 2004, p. 69). The multiple perspectives are a modernist image. At this time in Paris, from 1907 to 1917, Picasso was painting in his cubist style. With his artist friend, Budgen, Joyce debated whether *Ulysses* was more cubist or futurist in style, but Budgen thought cubist, especially the 'Cyclops' episode:

> Every event is a many-sided object. You first state one view of it and then you draw it from another angle to another scale, and both aspects lie side by side in the same picture.
>
> (1972, p. 75)

Budgen described Leopold Bloom as a sculpture in the Rodin sense: 'made of an infinite number of contours drawn from every conceivable angle' (*Ibid*, pp. 91–93).

In Trieste, Paris and Zurich, Joyce was at the heart of the avant-garde world and many of his contemporaries, especially composers, appear repeatedly in his work (McCreedy, 2018). Stravinsky, Schoenberg and Satie appear and in *Finnegans Wake* he mentions Shostakovich/'shattamovick', and Sibelius/'sibspecious' (FW 305). He understood complex music theory concepts, such as poly tonality and atonality, and was close friends with the modernist composers Phillipp Jarnach, Otto Luening and George Antheil, all of whom were directly involved in the artistic revolution. Joyce is also thought to have attended modern ballet performances of Stravinsky's *Rite of*

Spring, Schoenberg's *Erwartung* (1909), and Bartók's *Duke Bluebeard's Castle* (McCreedy, 1918).

For the composer Pierre Boulez, Joyce was a major literary influence. He saw Joyce as 'a key figure for the way in which avant-gardism in literature tended to precede avant-gardism in music' (1963). Avant-garde composer, John Cage, who was obsessed with Joyce and *Finnegans Wake* for much of his life, wrote the highly ambitious *Roaratorio, an Irish Circus on Finnegans Wake,* in 1979. Scott Klein says that although Joyce disliked most of the contemporary music of his day he was a central figure for the avant-garde composers, such as Luciano Berio, who gathered in Darmstadt after World War II (2004, part I).

Joyce may have been shy in the company of other avant-garde figures, but he would have kept in touch with all that was happening the same way he kept in touch with life back Dublin.

In the next and final chapter, we enter the world of the dream, the medieval/modernist *Finnegans Wake*.

References

Boulez, P. (1963). Sonate, Que me Veux-tu?, *Perspectives of New Music*, 1(2) (Spring, 1963): 32–44, Perspectives of New Music Publisher.

Budgen, F. (1972). *James Joyce and the Making of 'Ulysses'*. Oxford: Oxford UP.

Butler, C. (2004). Joyce the Modernist, *Cambridge Companion to James Joyce*, Cambridge: Cambridge University Press, pp. 67–86.

Chrisp, P. (2013). http://peterchrisp.blogspot.com/2013/12/the-book-of-kells.html

Klein, S. (2004). James Joyce and Avant-Garde Music, Contemporary Music Centre, Ireland, September. Available at www.cmc.ie/articles/article850.html. https://www.cmc.ie/features/james-joyce-and-avant-garde-music

Levin, H. (1960). *James Joyce*. London: New Directions.

McCreedy, J. (2018). James Joyce and 'Difficult Music': References to Modernist Classical Composers in *Finnegans Wake*. ENG 805: MA Dissertation.

Power, A. (1999). *Conversations with Joyce*. Dublin: The Lilliput Press. [Kindle Edition].

Toibin, C. (2012). *The Book of Kells* by Bernard Meehan—Review, *The Observer*, December.

11 *Finnegans Wake. The Poetry of the Dream*

'Quiet takes back her folded fields. Tranquille thanks. Adew'

In 1939, towards the end of his life and after 17 years immersed in *Finnegans Wake*, James Joyce wrote a moving final passage. It sounds like a mother speaking tenderly to her young son. The tone of the passage is in stark contrast to the searing entreaty, persecution and fury at his mother of his previous book, *Ulysses*, where he calls her 'ghoul, chewer of corpses!'. The simple writing style of this final passage is different from the linguistic play for which *Finnegans Wake* is famous. Joyce felt exhausted after he wrote it and sat for a long while on a street bench, unable to move. He had the passage read out to him that evening and it gave him great pleasure.

> …Come. Give me your great big hand for miny tiny. We will take our walk before they ring the bells. Not such big steps. It is hardly seven mile. It is very good for health in the morning. It seems so long since. As if you had been long far away. You will tell me some time if I can believe its all. You know where I am bringing you? You remember? Not a soul but ourselves. We might call on the Old Lord, what do you say? He is a fine sport. Remember to take off your white hat, eh? … I will tell you all sorts of stories, strange one. About every place we pass. It is all so often and still the same to me. Look! Your blackbirds! That's for your good luck. How glad you'll be I waked you. My! How well you'll feel. For ever after. First we turn a little here and then it's easy. I only hope the heavens sees us. A bit beside the bush and then a walk along the.
>
> (*JJ*, p. 713)

No longer all puns and parody, one is tempted to ask if this was the writing of James Joyce finally at peace with himself—the son reunited with his mother. Overwhelmed by the emotion, however, Joyce does not stay with the simplicity. He obscures it:

DOI: 10.4324/9781003309925-12

We might call on the Old Lord, what do you say? There's something tells me. He is a fine sport. Like the score and a moighty went before him. And a proper old promnentory. His door always open. For a newera's day. Much as your own is. You invoiced him last Eatster so he ought to give us hockockles and everything. Remember to take off your white hat, ech? When we come in the presence. And say hoothoothoo, ithmuthisthy! His is house of laws.

(FW, 623)

He then added a passage addressed to the troubled but charismatic father he loved. That Joyce should end his life's work with these intimate scenes of mother and son, and father and son, is very striking. This is the final passage:

And it's old and old it's sad and old it's sad and weary I go back to you, my cold father, my cold mad father, my cold mad feary father, till the near sight of the mere size of him, the moyles and moyles of it, moananoaning, makes me seasilt saltsick and I rush, my only, into your arms. I see them rising! Save me from those therrble prongs! Two more. Onetwo moremens more. So. Avelaval. My leaves have drifted from me.

All. But one clings still. I'll bear it on me. To remind me of. Lff!

So soft this morning, ours. Yes. Carry me along, taddy, like you done through the toy fair! If I seen him bearing down on me now under whitespread wings like he'd come from Arkangels, I sink I'd die down over his feet, humbly dumbly, only to washup. Yes,

tid. There's where. First. We pass through grass behush the bush to. Whish! A gull. Gulls. Far calls. Coming, far! End here. Us then. Finn, again! Take. Bussoftlhee, mememormee! Till thous- endsthee. Lps. The keys to. Given! A way a lone a last a loved a long the

(FW, 627–628)

The last sentence does not end, but circles back to the beginning of the book—Joyce re-immersing himself, circling back to Dublin and the all-embracing River Liffey, united with his parents in death.

The Story of Finnegans Wake

As with all of Joyce's work, the story in *Finnegans Wake* is of a family— the Earwicker family who lived at Chapelizod near Dublin. His own father is portrayed initially as a giant man stretched out across the north of Dublin from Howth to the Phoenix Park. As the story progresses, the father appears in different guises: as Humpty Dumpty, a publican—who has a great fall—as Finn MacCool, Tristram and finally as HCE, the Wake's 'most vital and polymorphous character' (Jackson and Costello, 1997, p. 427).

The book begins with the fall of the primordial giant Finnegan and his awakening as the modern family man and pub owner. The Prankquean Finnegan is a hod carrier who falls to his death while constructing a wall. His wife, Anna Livia Plurabelle, ALP, puts out his corpse as a meal for the mourners at his wake, but he vanishes before they can eat him. He is then seen sailing into Dublin Bay and rises to prominence as HCE 'Here Comes Everybody'.

He is brought low by a rumour concerning a sexual trespass, seen in Phoenix Park, apparently exhibiting himself to two innocent Irish girls. He is accused of every sin in the book, brought to trial, locked in prison, shoved into a coffin and buried deep under Lough Neagh. Olga Cox points out that 'If the facts of this story are uncertain, the tone of its telling is by turns accusatory and exculpatory, sounding always the keynote of guilt' (1993, p. 818).

A letter about him by his wife is called for as evidence. It was dictated to her son Shem, a writer (i.e. Joyce) and entrusted to her other son, postman Shaun, for delivery. The letter never arrives, ending up in a midden heap where it is unearthed by a hen.

Shaun slanders his brother, Shem, describing him as a forger and a 'sham'. Shem's mother defends him. There follows a chattering dialogue across the river by two washerwomen who as night falls become a tree and a stone. They gossip about ALP's response to the allegations laid against her husband and about her youthful affairs, before returning to the publication of HCE's guilt in the morning newspaper, and his wife's revenge on his enemies: borrowing a mailsack from her son Shaun the Post, she delivers presents to her 111 children.

The focus shifts to the children and their night letter to HCE and ALP, in which they are apparently united in a desire to overcome their parents.

HCE working in the pub is condemned by his customers and he delivers a confession of his crimes, including an incestuous desire for young girls. He morphs into ancient Irish high king Rory O'Connor and passes out. In his dream, four old men (Matthew, Mark, Luke and John) observe Tristan and Isolde and offer four commentaries on the lovers.

In the next part, Shaun, as postman, is having to deliver ALP's letter. Floating down the river Liffey in a barrel, he has posed 14 questions concerning the content of the letter. Shaun's answers focus on his own boastful personality and his admonishment of his artist brother, Shem. After the inquisition, Shaun loses his balance and the barrel careens over and he rolls backwards and disappears. He then re-appears and delivers a sexually suggestive sermon to his sister Issy. His father, HCE, then gives a defence of his own life in the passage 'Haveth Childers Everywhere'.

The parents attempt to copulate while their children are sleeping. One son has a nightmare of a scary father figure and the mother interrupts the coitus to go comfort him with the words 'You were dreamend, dear. The pawdrag? The fawthrig? Shoe! Hear are no phanthares in the room at all, avikkeen. No bad bold faathern, dear one'.

At the end, ALP becomes the river Liffey and disappears at dawn into the ocean. As Hugh Kenner puts it:

> In *Finnegans Wake*, [Joyce] broke the claustrophobic walls of the earlier drama, [*Ulysses*], to make a convincing superimposition of hilarity and pathos, the life of the family and the life of nations, Dublin politics and warring angelic powers, all educed from the human and therefore indefinitely capacious brain of a middle-aged father drowsing above his sawdust-strewn pub.
>
> (1956, p. 335)

Joyce may in real life have exiled himself from Dublin and his family, but he carried them with him and they were his subject.

Tindall calls *Finnegans Wake* a human comedy:

> His 'puntomime'. A master's play. Playing with everyone, everywhere, at every time, at the same time, like a juggler with eleven balls in the air...the Dublin talk of a triple thinker handles more than 'two thinks at a time'. A master Builder, above giddiness, he built a second and solider tower of 'Babbel' from the debris of the first (*Ulysses*).
>
> (1969, pp. 7–8)

Whereas in *Ulysses* he used Homer's *Odyssey* for a structure, *Finnegans Wake* follows the Oedipus story, plus Genesis, the Fall of Man and Redemption. It often refers back to *Ulysses* and the same themes run through both like Wagnerian leitmotifs. It is again a saga of guilt and confusion but somehow Joyce finds a new levity and poetry as well as connection, loyalty, love and forgiveness. The wifely/motherly devotion of ALP winds gently and reassuringly through the story. It could almost be called the return of the mother. Joyce may not have been able to talk about his mother after her death, but throughout *Finnegans Wake*, ALP is a constant stabilising and caring presence, 'the Allmaziful, the

Everliving, the Bringer of Plurabilities' (*FW*, p. 104). She is described in tender and intimate detail:

> Describe her! Hustle along, why can't you? Spitz on the iern ... the dearest little moma ever you saw nodding around her, all smiles, with ems of embarrass and aues to awe, between two ages, a judyqueen, not up to your ... She wore a ploughboy's nailstudded clogs, a pair of ploughfields in themselves: a sugarloaf hat with a gaudyquiviry peak and a band of gorse for an arnoment and a hundred streamers dancing off it and a guildered pin to pierce it: her bloodorange bockknickers, a two in one garment, showed natural nigger boggers, fancyfastened, free to undo. Hellsbells, I'm sorry I missed her!
>
> (*FW*, 207–208)

Another such description is of Anna's wedding preparations, which Edna O'Brien calls 'rapturous', 'belonging in the Song of Songs'. It begins:

> First she let her hair fall and down it flussed to her feet its teviots winding coils. Then, mothernakes, she sampood herself with galawater and fraguant pistania mud, wupper and lauar, from crown to sole ...
>
> (*FW*, 206)

In *Finnegans Wake,* HCE the husband/father is accused but, unexpectedly for one as persecuted as James Joyce, no serious evidence of guilt is found and Anna Livia caringly explains and defends him. Although still obsessive in his attempts to obscure emotion, what emerges is a new depressive position sense of emotional intimacy and connection with the world. As in all of Joyce's writing, we are still in Dublin but now there is a family at the centre and a new sense of belonging. The issue of belonging winds its way through Joyce's life. The replacement child can feel there is no place for them in their parents' eyes, or that they do not deserve to belong in the family when their sibling had died.

Dreamwork

> It is the poetry of the dream that catches and gives formal representation to the passions which are the meaning of our experience.
>
> (Meltzer)

Often in psychoanalysis, a new stage begins when patients become interested in their dreams and how the dreams relate to them. This facilitates a dialogue between patient and analyst and the work becomes a shared project. As Meltzer said, 'I feel pleasure and relief when a patient reports a dream...to tell a dream is an act of great confidentiality and inherent truthfulness' (2009, p. 133). For many patients, it is a magical time when they gradually discover the beauty of dreamwork. But for my two patients, their lives were still dominated by nightmares of dead babies, murder and monsters and, like Joyce, they felt implicated in the scenes of destruction. They felt helpless, dreading sleep, turning to alcohol. However, when they came to see the real impact of their childhood trauma, the nightmares miraculously disappeared, only reappearing occasionally in times of stress. While still frustrated with my separateness from her, my poet patient alluded to this turning point:

> Yet through those porcelain eyes, I shall put fire-lidded lions to rest:
> Through that parchment soul I shall resolve my foetus' guilt.
> (Already dead babies no longer flail against the surface of my dreams).

It is not clear whether Joyce's nightmares continued all his life, but perhaps locating *Finnegans Wake* in the world of the dream was an attempt to control them. His intense involvement in writing often late into the night could be Joyce trying to get the better of his own internal world—he would craft his own dreams:

> I reconstruct the nocturnal life as the Demiurge goes about the business of creation.
>
> (Mercanton, p. 209)

In *Finnegans Wake*, Joyce's imagination now has the freedom of the dreamworld—the immense freedom of the unconscious. Harry Levin, whose review of *Finnegans Wake* Joyce liked best and to whom he wrote warmly thanking him (*JJ*, p. 723), wrote:

> The dream convention is Joyce's licence for a free association of ideas and a systematic distortion of language. Psychoanalysis insinuates its special significances into his calculated slips of the tongue. Under cover of a drowsy indistinctness and a series of subconscious lapses, he has developed a diction that is actually alert and pointed, that bristles with virtuosity and will stoop to any kind of slapstick.
>
> (Levin, 1960, p. 185)

At the same time, Levin is taken aback by Joyce's attempts to obscure emotion:

> The nearer Joyce comes to a scene or an emotion, the more prone he is to indulge in literary by-play. When Earwicker's cri de coeur is muffled in a travesty of Macbeth, we may assume a studied evasion on the author's part, a determination to detach himself from his characters at all costs ... Joyce shows no more concern for his hero than a geneticist for a fruit-fly ... indifferent, he pares his fingernails, having reached the stage of artistic development that passes over the individual in favour of the general.
>
> (*Ibid*, p. 193)

As Devlin describes it:

> Language is put through a smeltingworks forever decomposed and recomposed. Broken down into bits that are then fused or 'coupled' into new elements, the words in the Wake are subjected to a process somewhat similar to the stewing of the relics in the midden: 'a bone, a pebble, a ramskin; chip them, chap them, cut them up allways; leave them to terracook in the muttheringpot' (*FW*, 20).
>
> (1991, p. 12)

Trying to manage the emotion, Joyce uses all the Freudian mechanisms of displacement, condensation, substitution, wordplay and allusion. Walton Litz (1961, p. 123) wonders if it is new techniques rather than new experience which give his work its life. It seems also that the new techniques keep him alive. They distract from his experience which threatens to overwhelm him, as he remains 'a paper leaf away from madness'. Lacan suggested Joyce interposed the writing of *Finnegans Wake* between himself and an encounter with unbearable, perhaps psychotic, anxiety (Cox, 1993, p. 819). One visitor to Joyce in Paris found him disturbed that a passage in Finnegans Wake was 'still not obscure enough'. His solution was to add words from the language of the Samoyedic peoples of Siberia! But all the while, in his final work, Joyce was carefully mending this broken Dublin family and the intimate connection between them.

Joyce working to distract from his emotional pain is different from a denial of life events and 'turning a blind eye' that I have described elsewhere (Adams, 1999). Although fearing rejection and condemnation, Joyce does want to know and to understand.

When Meltzer talks about the 'poetry' of the dream, he has in mind the capacity of a dream to give shape to emotional experience the way poetry can. It has been said that one way to read *Finnegans Wake* is to give it the same close attention that one would a poem. 'It is not only to be read. It is to be looked at and listened to' (Beckett et al., 1929, p. 14).

Anna Livia Plurabelle

'The heart bows down'

Anthony Burgess, exclaims about *Anna Livia Plurabelle*:

> When we have doubts about the value of *Finnegans Wake*...we have only to think of the wonderful final [*Anna Livia*] chapter of Book One for the doubts to be resolved. It remains one of the most astonishing pieces of audacity in the whole of world literature, and the audacity comes off. The language is cosmic, yet it is the homely speech of ordinary people. We seem to see a woman who is also a river and a man who is also a city. Time dissolves; we have a glimpse of eternity. And the eternal vision is made out of muddy water, old saws, half-remembered music-hall songs, gossip, and the stain on a pair of underpants. The heart bows down.
>
> (1965, p. 218)

This section about the gossiping washerwomen is an example of Joyce's interweaving myth and political reality—as well as a sensitivity to their hardship. It has the charm of Homer's Odysseus encountering Nausicaa and her washerwomen, and the Minyeides episode in Ovid's *Metamorphoses* (*Met.* 4.1–415), in which three sisters entertain each other as they work by telling stories until Bacchus arrives at dusk and transforms them into bats and their work into vines. The political reality, however, was the oppression of the many Irish washerwomen barred from joining a union. Joyce was aware of this reality. At University, he was close friends with Francis Sheehy Skeffington, brother of the famous Irish suffragette, Hanna, who in 1911 organised the Irish Women Workers' Union. In a tribute to their toil, he ends the section with the two washerwomen saying their talk 'saved' them and how tired and 'heavy as yonder stone' they are at the end of the day's washing:

> Ho, talk save us! My foos won't moos. I feel as old as yonder elm. A tale told of Shaun or Shem? All Livia's daughter-sons. Dark hawks hear us. Night! Night! My ho head halls. I feel as heavy as yonder

stone. Tell me of John or Shaun? Who were Shem and Shaun the living sons or daughters of? Night now! Tell me, tell me, tell me, elm! Night night! Telmetale of stem or stone. Beside the rivering waters of, hitherandthithering waters of. Night!

(FW, 215–216)

Edna O'Brien describes how Joyce wrote seven versions of this chapter, constituting thousands of hours of labour, 'each episode more enriched, more exuberant and more transmutative'. The *Anna Livia* section begins in a gay, effervescent mood, as two washerwomen on opposite sides of the River Liffey regale each other with scathing gossip:

> The sounds are of water, birdsong, bird cries, the beating of the battler on convent napkins, baby shawls, combies and sheets that a man and his bride embraced on. So they tuck up their sleeves, loosen the 'talk-tapes' and egg each other on to tell it 'in franca lingua. And call a spate a spate'. We are introduced to Anna, a shy, limber slip of a thing, 'in Lapsummer skirt and damazon cheeks', her hair down to her feet, 'her little mary' washed in bog water, with amulets of rhunerhinerstones around her neck.

(O'Brien, 2017, p. viii)

> O
> tell me all about
> Anna Livia! I want to hear all

about Anna Livia. Well, you know Anna Livia? Yes, of course, we all know Anna Livia. Tell me all. Tell me now. You'll die when you hear. Well, you know, when the old cheb went futt and did what you know. Yes, I know, go on. Wash quit and don't be dabbling. Tuck up your sleeves and loosen your talktapes. And don't butt me—hike!—when you bend. Or whatever it was they threed to make out he thried to two in the Fiendish park. He's an awful old reppe. Look at the shirt of him! Look at the dirt of it! He has all my water black on me. And it steeping and stuping since this time last wik. How many goes is it I wonder I washed it? I know by heart the places he likes to saale, duddurty devil! Scorching my hand and starving my famine to make his private linen public. Wallop it well with your battle and clean it. My wrists are wrusty rubbing the mouldaw stains. And the dneepers of wet and the gangres of sin in it!

(FW, 196–216)

Overwhelmed by its extraordinary music, Joyce's friend, Mercanton wrote:

> [It is] like a sort of mystical chant, so sharp, so spare, so shimmering, such as I had perceived in no other poetry. …nothing could be more opposite to an intoxication of the spirit, or to a hallucination of the sense and of the soul than this patiently explored dream. This great virtuoso of language, endowed with all the tricks and subtleties of his craft, was sincere. There is a Joycean tone that is like no other: mysterious moral beauty in a universe of pure idea.
>
> (1979, pp. 209–210)

In *Ulysses*, the tragedy of Molly and Bloom's son's death is central but, as with the trauma of the Irish Famine, it is surrounded by silence and paralysis. In *Finnegans Wake*, however, the same themes return but with a new expressive freedom. The mothers are still 'crippled with children', but a passage about the lost child, Anna's 'firstborn and firstfruit of woe', is in a different realm:

> and lo, you're doomed, joyday dawns and….it is to you, firstborn and firstfruit of woe, to me, branded sheep, pick of the wasterpaperbaskel, by the tremours of Thundery and Ulerin's dogstar, you alone, windblasted tree of the knowledge of beautiful andevil…. because ye left from me, because ye laughted on me, because, O me lonely son, ye are forgetting me!
>
> (*FW*, 194)

The Irish Famine appears with new intensity throughout *Finnegans Wake*:

> Repopulate the land of your birth and count up your progeny by the hungered head and the angered thousand.
>
> (*FW*, 188)

Usurpers and changelings appear as the rival twins, Shem and Shaun—but they become magically reconciled and as one. HCE envisions himself forgotten and unmissed because he senses that he may be replaced by another:

> For, be that samesake sibsubstitute of a hooky salmon, there's already a big rody ram lad at randome on the premises of his haunt of the hungred bordles, as it is told me. Shop Illicit, flourishing like a lordmajor or a buaboabaybohm.
>
> (*FW*, 28–29)

Guilt and condemnation are still pervasive. According to Kenner, 'the emotion in *Finnegans Wake* is contained in the permanent plight of the unmoving Earwicker, recumbent prey of many inner voices; the battle of self with shadow-self' (1956, p. 357). Anthony Burgess wrote:

> HCE has, so deep is his sleep, sunk to a level of dreaming in which he has become a collective being rehearsing the collective guilt of man. Man falls, man rises so that he can fall again.
>
> (2011, p. i)

Joyce saw himself as a 'Melancholy Jesus' and a 'Crooked Jesus' (O'Toole, 2012, p. 46). As Shem, the brother, he is a 'sham' and a fraudster. As already mentioned, Joyce's court room scenes of accusation, in both *Ulysses* and *Finnegans Wake,* convey the poignant fears of the replacement child as usurper, haunted by dread and persecution. But the misdemeanours in *Finnegans Wake* are viewed with great compassion and as all too human. HCE is neither condemned nor convicted.

Seamus Heaney paid an extraordinary tribute to the new freedom in Joyce, 'Joyce, the great and true liberator', in his 1984 *Station Island* poem. Heaney would have been 45 at the time. In the final part (section XII), the returning pilgrim encounters a ghost who turns out to be James Joyce himself. Joyce says to him, 'the main thing is to write for the joy of it. …You are fasted now, light-headed, dangerous. Take off from here. …Let go, let fly, forget. …Now strike your note' (1998, p. 267). Heaney himself felt new freedom, as well as guilt, after leaving Northern Ireland for County Wicklow when he was 33. He well understood Joyce's need for the spaciousness of exile to escape the Dublin grief, paralysis and oppression. But this tribute goes deeper than mere identification and conveys both love and admiration.

In later life, with the constant presence of his wife Nora, Joyce seemed to experience a new sense of belonging and intimacy within his family and his circle of friends in exile. He was able to share personal joy as well as regrets and fears and shed tears. He would have been at the centre without feeling like a usurper. In making *Finnegans Wake* a tribute to his father and by resurrecting his mother, he was also giving meaning and worth to his own existence, becoming a legitimate son.

Conclusion

'Quiet takes back her folded fields. Tranquille thanks. Adew'.

(*FW*)

Joyce liked to remind himself that he had begun Finnegans Wake in his mid-30s, 'the same age as Dante when he started his great *Divine Comedy* and Shakespeare wrestled with his Dark Lady of the sonnets' (O'Brien, 1999, p. 93). Joyce felt an affinity with Shakespeare (as seen throughout *Ulysses*) in a shared early abandonment by the mother. After the striking absence of mothers in Shakespeare's plays, in his late play, *The Winter's Tale*, there is a mother, Hermione, who, like Anna Livia in *Finnegans Wake*, is brought back to life. Having been turned to stone for some 16 years, Hermione is suddenly alive: 'O, she's warm!', cries Leontes.

The *Winter's Tale* is harrowing in its portrayal of intense jealousy, feelings which also threatened to cripple Joyce, as seen in his letters to Nora. Leontes' jealousy is as much about mother's 'other babies'—the son, Mamillius, and the daughter, Perdita, who he disowns and casts away:

> This brat is none of mine;
> It is the issue of Polixenes:
> Hence with it, and together with the dam
> Commit them to the fire!
> The bastard brains with these my proper hands
> Shall I dash out.
> bear it
> To some remote and desert place quite out
> Of our dominions, and that there thou leave it,
> Without more mercy, to its own protection
> And favour of the climate.
>   (Act 2, scene III)

We also feel Leontes' delusional jealousy towards his friend, his 'twin', Polixenes: 'We were as twinn'd lambs that did frisk i' th' sun' (Act 1, II). There is the inevitable court scene that goes with the paranoid world and the wife/mother is condemned. However, there follows a dreamlike other world episode located in 'Bohemia', full of fun and new life. James Fisher sees this as a picture of a transformation in Leontes' internal world leading to remorse and restitution (1999, p. 24). This could also be a description of *Finnegans Wake* with its liveliness and new forgiveness.

Joyce's characters do not rage and agonise as they do in Shakespeare's plays. They do not act out their sorrow. Instead, Joyce pulls at us by the music of his writing and the pathos of the situation. In *Finnegans Wake,* he tries to obscure the emotional intensity by grinding up words and 'spinning subtle and complicated cobwebs out of his own tortured entrails' (Levin).

Dante's quest and journey seem of a different order to Joyce's, even though he too was steeped in grief for the loss of his beloved and his homeland. Dante seemed on a spiritual search for meaning and human understanding compared perhaps with Joyce's struggle to survive an inner world of guilt and persecution. Dante's exile was forced on him, whereas Joyce's lifelong exile seemed an attempt at freeing himself from a claustrum-like internal world, often linked in his mind with Catholic Ireland.

Sigmund Freud felt a new freedom after his mother died, but he was already elderly. Like Joyce, Freud's last years involved considerable physical suffering which he, too, endured with great strength and dignity (Schur, 1972). Unlike Joyce, however, he remained cut off from his dependent, 'feminine' self, surrounding himself for comfort with his collection of antiquities. His last writing, *Moses and Monotheism,* while representing a return to Judaism and the father, has no Anna Livia carrying him back home, nor the playful release from persecution.

It is unclear how much Joyce felt a sense of resolution in life. But he did seem to feel he had a place in the world, so important for a replacement child. In his state of physical decline and exhaustion, he sought solace imagining a return to his homeland and fusion with his parents. At the end, before addressing his 'cold mad feary father', he 'lilted' this gentle farewell. *Finnegans Wake* had carried him safely to the end:

> Be happy, dear ones! May I be wrong! For she'll be sweet for you as I was sweet when I came down out of me mother. My great blue bedroom, the air so quiet, scarce a cloud. In peace and silence. I could have stayed up there for always only ... let her rain for my time is come. I done me best when I was let. Thinking always if I go all goes ... How small it's all! And me letting on to meself always. And lilting on all the time. I thought you were all glittering with the noblest of carriage. You're only a bumpkin ... Loonely in me loneness. For all their faults. I am passing out. O bitter ending! I'll slip away before they're up. They'll never see. Nor know. Nor miss me.
>
> (*FW*, 627)

References

Adams, M. (1999). "Turning a Blind Eye': Misrepresentation and the Denial of Life Events', in S. Ruszczynski and S. Johnson, eds., *Psychoanalytic Psychotherapy in the Kleinian Tradition*, London: Karnac Books, pp. 75–92.

Beckett, S., et al. (1929). *Our Exagmination Round His Factification for Incamination of* Work in Progress. London: Faber & Faber, 1972.

Burgess, A. (1965). *Here Comes Everybody: An Introduction to James Joyce for the Ordinary Reader.* London: Faber and Faber.

Burgess, A. (2011). *Finnegans Wake: What's It All about?* http://www.metaportal.com.br/jjoyce/burgess1.htm

Cox, O. (1993). Some Dream Mechanisms in Finnegans Wake, *International Journal of Psycho-Analysis*, 74: 815–821.

Devlin, K. J. (1991). *Wandering and Return in Finnegans Wake: An Integrative Approach to Joyce's Fictions.* Princeton, NJ: Princeton Legacy Library, PUP.

Fisher, J. V. (1999). *The Uninvited Guest. Emerging from Narcissism towards Marriage.* London: Karnac Books.

Heaney, S. (1998). *Opened Ground: Poems 1966–1996.* London: Faber & Faber.

Jackson, J. W., & Costello, P. (1997). *John Stanislaus Joyce: The Voluminous Life and Genius of James Joyce's Father.* London: Fourth Estate.

Joyce, J. (2012 edition). *Finnegans Wake,* ed. F. Fordham et al. Oxford World Classics, OUP, Oxford.

Kenner, H. (1956). *Dublin's Joyce.* Boston, MA: Beacon Press.

Litz, A. W. (1961). *The art of James Joyce. Method and Design in Ulysses and Finnegans Wake.* Oxford: Oxford UP.

Meltzer, D. (2009). *Dream Life: A Re-Examination of the Psychoanalytic Theory and Technique.* Karnac (The Harris Meltzer Trust Series).

O'Brien, E. (2017). *Foreword to Anna Livia Plurabelle.* London: Faber & Faber.

O'Toole, F. (2012). *Joyce: Heroic, Comic. The New York Review of Books*, October 25.

Schur, M. (1972). *Freud: Living and Dying.* New York: International Universities Press.

Shakespeare, W. (1994) *The Winter's Tale,* Arden Shakespeare, J. Pafford, ed. London: Routledge.

Tindall, W. Y. (1969). *A Reader's Guide to Finnegans Wake.* Syracuse, NY: Syracuse University.

Appendix
Other Notable Replacement Children

Given the prevalence of child mortality, it is not surprising that many famous people experienced the loss of siblings. Pollock has noted that over 1,000 writers have experienced a significant object loss during childhood: 'A close relationship has been established between early trauma, object loss and creativity with the creative work a means of achieving narcissistic repair and making restitution' (Kligerman, 1972). I list below some of our better-known artists and writers who lost siblings in childhood.

PLAYWRIGHTS: Shakespeare; Anton Chekov; Henrik Ibsen; Sean O'Casey; Eugene O'Neil; Arthur Schnitzler; August Strindberg; David Storey; Thornton Wilder
WRITERS: Balzac; Barrie; Kafka; Kerouac; Edward Said; Stendhal; Beecher Stowe
POETS: Louise Glück; T. S. Eliot; Goethe; Mallarme; Milton; Rilke; W. B. Yeats; William Blake
MUSICIANS: Beethoven; Mahler; Mozart; Verdi; Schoenberg
PAINTERS: Dali; Kollwitz; Matisse; Rothko; Van Gogh, Louise Bourgeois

William Blake (1757–1827) English Poet & Painter

'O why was I born with a different face?'

William Blake had six siblings, two of whom died in infancy. Like Joyce, Blake was born after his parents lost their firstborn son. But unlike Joyce who was the favoured son, Blake's next brother was the favoured one, named John after the lost first child. To the end of his life, Blake remembered how his parents favoured a younger brother. Blake called him 'the evil one'.

Although his parents recognised and encouraged Blake's talents, he led a solitary childhood. Peter Ackroyd writes:

> He might have been some star-child, or changeling, who withdrew into himself and into his own myth because he could not deal directly or painlessly even with the human beings closest to him. Certainly, part of the momentum of his great epic poetry derives from his need single-handedly to create a new inheritance and a new genealogy for himself. Yet there may be anxiety and guilt attendant upon such a pursuit, and the sense of separation may lead to the threat of punishment.
>
> (1995, pp. 7–8)

This is reminiscent of Stephen in *Ulysses* wanting the son to be his own father (U, p. 46). Richard Holmes writes: Blake appears to have been largely indifferent to the rest of his siblings:

> A man's worst enemies are those
> Of his own house and family.

The family itself was to be banished from his life and from his memory (2015, p. 4).

In his poetry fathers are slain, mothers are weak or faithless and 'soft Family-Love' is denounced (*Ibid*, p. 8). Their myths present 'profound insights into the divided self, a condition that many people experience to some extent and that Blake experienced to a terrifying degree' (*Ibid*).

Like Joyce, Blake was extremely bright, impressionable and had a highly active imagination. As a child, his closest and most significant attachment was to the Bible. This brings to mind Joyce's immersion in the *Book of Kells* and Freud's in the Philippson Bible. All his life, from early childhood, Blake had visions—at four he saw God 'put his head to the window'; around age nine, while walking through the countryside, he saw a tree filled with angels. One wonders how much awareness of the first son having died contributed to these visions. Children appear in his poetry: 'spirited, enraged or simply afraid' (Ackroyd, p. 10). Were his visions comparable to Joyce's nightmares?

He seems never to have forgiven his mother and believed Christ 'took much after his Mother. And in so far he was one of the worst of men' (*Ibid*, p. 9).

In old age he tried to read the parable of the Prodigal Son, but broke down and wept when he came to the passage, 'When he was yet a great way off, his father saw him'. It was as if he were then confronting the nature of his own life for the first time.

Like Joyce, he had a devoted wife, but his Catherine was no Nora. Nora had a mind of her own and stood up to Joyce. Catherine remarked: 'I have very little of Mr. Blake's company, he is always in Paradise'.

> She would get up in the night, when he was under his very fierce inspirations, which were as if they would tear him asunder.... She had to sit motionless and silent, only to stay him mentally, without moving hand or foot; this for hours, and night after night.
>
> (Holmes, 2015)

Shakespeare (1564–1616)

Shakespeare's mother, Mary, lost three daughters and her second one only three months before Shakespeare was conceived. Donald Silver, who has written compellingly about the effect of sibling loss on Shakespeare, speculates that if Mary was melancholic during his infancy, the youthful Shakespeare presumably came to view all mothers in terms of the depressive environment of his upbringing. Silver focuses on the autobiographical meaning of *The Sonnets* by demonstrating how their imagery and special tone reflect the experiences of loss and mourning that typified Shakespeare's early life.

> In Sonnet 143, it is not difficult to imagine the boy Shakespeare speaking poignantly from within himself to the mother of his past who, having lost three daughters, mourned for them to the point of neglecting her eldest son. In a more contemporary clinical idiom, the sonnet could be entitled, 'Ode to a Replacement Child', because it so tellingly depicts the fate of such a child.
>
> (Silver, 1983)

With the exception of one, all of the daughters died. One year after the death of the second daughter, William was born. He was their oldest living child as well as their oldest son. His mother gave birth to three other sons after William.

Grieving mothers and 'three sisters' and themes of death and mourning recur throughout Shakespeare's plays. Richard III has three lamenting queens who chant their grief, not so much for their lost spouses as for their lost children. Three deathlike witches haunt Macbeth. In King John, a play inspired by the recent loss of his own son, Hamnet,

Shakespeare depicts a mother raging at 'death' stealing upon her son. She begs death to snatch her instead from this world:

> Death, death:—O, amiable lovely death!
> Thou odoriferous stench! sound rottenness!
> Arise forth from the couch of lasting night,
> Thou hate and terror to prosperity,
> And I will kiss thy detestable bones,
> And put my eyeballs in the vaulty brows,
> And ring these fingers with thy household worms;
> And stop this gap of breath with fulsome dust,
> And be a carrion monster like thyself;
> Come, grin on me; and I will think thou smil'st
> And buss thee as thy wife! Misery's love,
> O, come to me!
> > (III, 4)

In Sonnet 143, the 'mother's' attention is turned away from the poet by her yearning for those she has lost, represented by the birds that Shakespeare frequently used to symbolize children. Even in the context of his profound disappointment, he urges her to be gentle and to return her attention to him:

> Lo, as a careful housewife runs to catch
> One of her feather'd creatures broke away,
> Sets down her babe, and makes all swift dispatch
> In pursuit of the thing she would have stay;
> Whilst her neglected child holds her in chase,
> Cries to catch her whose busy care is bent
> To follow that which flies before her face,
> Not prizing her poor infant's discontent.
> So runn'st thou after that which flies from thee,
> Whilst I thy babe chase thee afar behind;
> But if thou catch thy hope, turn back to me,
> And play the mother's part, kiss me, be kind.
> So will I pray that thou mayst have thy Will,
> If thou turn back, and my loud crying still.

John Milton (1608–1674) English Poet

Milton was two years old in 1610 when his maternal grandmother, who lived with the family, died. When Milton was three, his baby sister,

Sara, died and when seven, his infant sister Tabitha. In 1638, seven months after the death of his mother, when the poet was 30, *Lycidas* was published. In grieving for his mother, it is likely that earlier unresolved deaths were reawakened, possibly stimulating the creation of *Lycidas*. In her 1993 paper, Wanamaker writes:

> Typically, the anger is projected against mother figures in the poem…which only strengthens my feeling that it is ultimately the baby sisters' deaths with which Milton struggles most. …He puts the blame on their mother. Why wasn't she taking better care of them? How could she let them die? It was her fault, not mine.
>
> (p. 588)

She also talks of Milton's 'twin drive for fame and the elimination of rivals':

> At times Milton's poetic gift seems to depend almost proportionally on the magnitude of his imagined persecution and hatred of rivals. In some of the poem's loveliest lines, Milton confronts the loss of Lycidas, but always in the shadows …those first losses. 'But O the heavy change, now thou art gone/Now thou art gone, and never must return!'
>
> (pp. 591–592)

His preoccupation with guilt, probably deriving in part from the incompletely resolved childhood deaths, continued to haunt him. It may well have contributed to the genesis of his greatest work of all, *Paradise Lost* (1674), which ultimately is more about resolving loss and guilt than anything else (p. 599).

Sean O'Casey (1880–1964) Irish Playwright

The youngest of 13 children, O'Casey was born in the Dublin tenements to a Catholic father and Protestant mother in whose religion he was raised. Three of his siblings had died. His father died when he was three and the large family survived on dry bread and tea. He taught himself to read when he was 14 but had no normal education. In his six-part autobiography, he describes in heart-wrenching detail his mother's experiences of giving birth and then losing children. For example:

> She would never have another child…He died of the same thing died of croup…He had been vigorous enough and had sprawled and kicked a twelve month way into the world.

But he got ill and she rushed him all the way to the hospital. Then back home with him dead in her arms...The third Johnny crawled a little further into life (O'Casey, 2011).

Ludwig Van Beethoven (1770–1827) German Composer

> Two Souls, alas are dwelling in my heart.

Similar to James Joyce, a year before Beethoven's birth, a brother was born who lived for only six days. Ludwig was given the same name as the lost brother. His mother then had five more children in the space of six years, three of whom died. Beethoven was very aware of his lost brother and suffered great inner torment, anger and loneliness. Unlike Joyce, who had the support and devotion of his wife, Nora, Beethoven never managed to create a sense of belonging or a family for himself. Beethoven's late works are described by Solomon:

> It is as if the earlier extrovert has turned inward, and now produces gnarled and eccentric pieces of music that make unprecedented demands on performer and listener alike, and at the same time convey a sense not of resignation but of an unusual rebelliousness, breaking barriers, transgressively exploring the basic elements of the art as if anew.
>
> (1975)

Salvador Dali (1904–1989) Spanish Painter

Dalí's older brother, who had also been named Salvador, died of gastroenteritis nine months before Dali was born. Dalí was haunted by the idea of his dead brother throughout his life, mythologizing him in his writings and art: '[we] resembled each other like two drops of water, but we had different reflections'. Images of his brother reappeared in his later works, including *Portrait of My Dead Brother*.

(Hartman, 2008)

Johann Wolfgang Von Goethe (1749–1832) German Poet

Goethe, a hero of Freud's, lost four siblings. In 'A Childhood Recollection from Dichtung und Wahrheit' (1917), Freud interpreted a childhood memory of Goethe's, throwing crockery out of the window, as his wish to get rid of a disturbing intruder: 'the new baby must be rid of—through the window' (Pollock, 1978, p. 476). Goethe's *Erlkonig* poem is a most powerful story of a baby's death and he shares with Freud a lifelong fascination with Moses, the child who survived.

Henrik Ibsen (1828–1906) Norwegian Playwright

'I didn't ask to be born' [from *Ghosts*]

James Joyce's great hero, Ibsen, was also a replacement child. A month after his birth, his 18-month-old brother died. Just like Joyce, Ibsen's parents had lost their firstborn son. His mother then gave birth to three more sons and a daughter. Having previously been a lively woman with a passionate interest in the theatre, Ibsen's mother became a withdrawn and melancholy recluse.

As I discuss in Chapter 1, the Kleinian analyst, Joan Riviere, herself a replacement child, wrote a paper on the lost child in Ibsen's *Masterbuilder* (1952).

Franz Kafka (1883–1924) Czech Novelist

Franz Kafka was the firstborn child. The two boys born after Franz did not survive: Georg died of measles when he was 15 months old, and the next-born, Heinrich, lived only six months before succumbing to meningitis. The parents then had three daughters, all of whom survived. Banville quotes Reiner Stach about Kafka's childhood:

> These constant fluctuations resulted not only in an atmosphere of tumult and frayed nerves, but also in a series of separations that instilled in little Franz a deep mistrust regarding the consistency of human relationships and wariness of a world in which every face he had become accustomed to or even grown to love could vanish instantly and forever.

Banville asks:

> 'How did this couple beget a son so delicately made, so tall, and thin to the point of emaciation? It is as if this singular creature were his own self-creation'. For a person as sensitive as Kafka, or at least as he presented himself as being …inner escape was the only available strategy. If we are to believe his own personal mythology, he

drifted out of life and into literature, to the point, indeed, that as an adult he would declare that he *was* literature, and nothing else.

(Banville, 2017)

Kathe Kollwitz (1867–1945) German Artist

Käthe Kollwitz was one of four siblings to live beyond childhood. Her mother's first two children died at a very early age and her last-born child, a son, died of meningitis when he was one year old. Alice Miller (1990) wrote that reading Kollwitz' diaries after viewing the paintings enabled her to understand why the paintings seemed so overwhelmingly depressing. Capps wrote:

> The paintings depict dead children and an older woman who entrusts herself to death, and contrasts the feelings the mother has toward her dead child and her living children. The living children 'must be dutifully cared for and raised in a way to rid them of their bad behavior and make them acceptable in the future', and this being the case, 'to be too affectionate would be dangerous, for too much love could ruin them'. It's a different matter in the case of her dead child, 'for that child needs nothing from her and does not awaken any feelings of inferiority or hatred, does not cause her any conflict, does not offend her'. And since she need not be afraid of spoiling the child with her love, 'when she goes to the cemetery she feels genuine inner freedom in her grief'.
>
> (Capps, 2012, p. 28)

The oldest of her siblings was Konrad; two other children born earlier than Konrad had died. Next came Julie, then Käthe, then Lise, and finally Benjamin, who was the youngest but who died at one year of age from meningitis when Käthe was about 11.

> Memories of Benjamin's illness and death were deeply stamped on Käthe's mind. As a mature woman and even in her old age she recalled how she ached with love and pity as her reserved mother grieved silently for Benjamin. More than one great work of Käthe's was to embody such desperate, helpless grief. Others reversed the roles with the living child clinging to the mother threatened by death.
>
> (Klein and Klein, 1975, p. 6)

Marie-Henri Stendhal (1783–1842) French Writer

Henri Beyle [Stendhal] was a replacement child, born into a family with a grieving mother. He was given the same name as the child who died a year earlier. He saw another sibling die, and then lost his mother at the age of seven.

> He seems to have suffered from depression and perhaps, hypomania, which affected the 'starts' and 'stops' of his writing. It's been suggested that *Henry Brulard's Life* is an autobiography that also served as a kind of personal analysis. Perhaps Stendhal didn't feel that he had the right to exist on his own terms and that he was condemned to 'not-be'. As for many replacement children, Stendhal felt that he was supposed to be his little deceased brother, at least from his parent's perspective.
>
> (Wilson, 1988)

The theme of the child recurs throughout Stendhal's work: pregnancy and the unborn child, childbirth, the child that has died, the endangered child and the illegitimate child. Wilson points to the replacement child's literary device of the pseudonym.

> According to Stendhal, you receive a pseudonym as a replacement child, since the name given to you doesn't really belong to you, but rather to your predecessor. Perhaps, Stendhal was attempting to 'self-create'—to both 'name' himself and to create and assume an identity of his own. And ultimately, Stendhal did achieve acclaim and a name for himself, and an identity uniquely his own.
>
> (Ibid)

August Strindberg (1849–1912) Swedish Playwright

August Strindberg's life was permeated by loss. When he was 12, his mother died of tuberculosis. Earlier, four infant siblings had died. Later, his own first child died two days after birth. The failure of three marriages and loss of contact with the children of these marriages profoundly depressed him. Burnham (1996) writes:

> His losses engendered a lifelong sense of separation and alienation. He was an 'outsider' who, though fiercely and defiantly proud of his singularity and difference from the crowd, yearned ceaselessly for a respected place in the social order, for communion with

his fellow beings. In his isolation he felt himself to be a cursed outcast, a homeless wanderer, like the Wandering Jew or the Flying Dutchman. Loss of community was a torment and a dominant force throughout his life.

Vincent Van Gogh (1853–1890) Dutch Painter

Of great importance in Vincent's life was his role as a replacement child. Not only was he born one year to the day after the stillborn death of a brother on March 30, 1853, and not only was he given the exact same name, but he probably also frequently saw the gravestone with his own name inscribed. Thus, he began life with a birth/death theme (Friedman, 1999).

Thornton Wilder (1897–1975) American Writer. 'The twinless twin'

Thornton Wilder's twin brother died at birth. Like many twinless twins, this was a death event which haunted him for most of his life. Repeatedly, in Wilder's works one finds the theme of death, trying to understand death from the point of view of the dead and communication with the dead. He spent a lifetime searching for the part of him that was missing. His emotional reactions to his successes were pure guilt: after winning his first Pulitzer Prize, he felt 'a glib and graceful hypocrisy' begin to emerge within him. He retreated to his mother to be 'cured' and said of his sense of loneliness in the world, 'I don't belong'. In his journals, begun at age 15, he ruminated incessantly on the theme of his twin as a driving force in his creative life (Glenn, 1986).

W B Yeats 1865–1939 Irish Poet

When he was eight, Yeats' three-year-old brother died and he was 10 when his sister died. This is the first stanza of one of his most famous poems, *The Stolen Child* (1886):

> Where dips the rocky highland
> Of Sleuth Wood in the lake,
> There lies a leafy island
> Where flapping herons wake
> The drowsy water rats;
> There we've hid our faery vats,
> Full of berrys

And of reddest stolen cherries.
Come away, O human child!
To the waters and the wild
With a faery, hand in hand,
For the world's more full of weeping than you can understand.

Gustav Mahler (1860–1911) Austrian Composer

Of the 12 children born to Mahler's parents only six survived infancy. The winter following Gustav's fifth birthday brought the twin deaths two months apart of the two youngest brothers, Karl and Rudolph, age 16 months and 6 months, respectively. More siblings were born when Gustav was seven (Alois), eight (Justine) and nine (Arnold). The last died while the now 11-year-old Gustav was spending six months in Prague. While he was away, another child had been born (Friedrich) and still another (Alfred) came the following year. Otto, the last boy, later to reveal severe mental disturbance and to emulate Gustav in aspiring to become a musician and composer, was born under sad circumstances when Gustav was 13 years old, barely a month after the death of the infant, Alfred. As Feder describes it:

> The sibling Gustav was closest to and with whom a tender relationship seemed to have developed was the sickly Ernst, who was less than one year his junior. Ernst's lingering death, of rheumatic heart disease, finally occurred on what was probably his 13th birthday. It was Gustav's great adolescent sorrow and represented for him the end of childhood. But in February of 1889, while Mahler was still in Budapest, his father died, followed by his mother in October. Leopoldine, who would have been the oldest responsible sister for a growing brood, had died of a brain tumour only a month earlier, and so the 29-year-old bachelor musician found himself in the unwelcome and unaccustomed role of head of a family in another part of Europe.
>
> (1978, p. 128)

Henri Matisse (1869–1954) French Painter

Henri-Émile Benoît Matisse was the firstborn son. The second son, Émile-Auguste, was born in 1872, but died before he was two. Two months after his death while still mourning for her dead son, Anna bore her last baby and third son. He was given the reversal of the dead infant's name, Auguste-Émile. This reversal of the name of the dead child for the succeeding one may have caused uncomfortable reverberations within the delicate Henri. The birth of his second brother and rival, this baby's subsequent death, perhaps unconsciously desired by the elder brother, and seemingly quick replacement, surely caused anxiety for the infant Henri. He was faced with survivor guilt, distrust about the invulnerability of his own body, as well as apprehension about the potential substitution in the affections of his parents should another child be born. The mother's preoccupation with illness, birth and death of one of her three babies in five years must have resulted in a prolonged period of emotions, joy, sorrow and fatigue with alternate withdrawal and protective behaviour towards her two remaining children (Ravenal, 1995).

Louise Bourgeois (1911–2010) French artist/sculptor

Meg Harris Williams writes:

> Our picture of Louise as a child is that she was the darling of the family – clever, pretty, dependable - yet full of fears about the damage caused by her own greed, possessiveness and competitiveness. Bright and healthy herself she nonetheless felt herself to be a victim, 'abandoned', 'little orphan Annie', identified with a baby sister who had died. (2010)

Bourgeois described having crushing anxiety attacks, four times a day, all her life. She was in analysis with Henry Lowenfeld from 1952 to 1982 but this seems another example of the analysis not having explored the trauma of losing her sister. She herself said: 'The truth is that Freud did nothing for artists, or for the artist's problem, the artist's torment.'

An *ArtLyst* article in 2012 describes fear being the main theme of her work, along with anger. "I have fantastic pleasure in breaking everything," she said, but mostly the violence is in her work. In one celebrated piece, a six-foot marble statue called "She-Fox" (1985), the animal has been decapitated, and there is a big gash in its throat. At the base of the statue, huddling behind the animal's haunches, is a tiny female figure. Bourgeois has explained that the she-fox is her mother and the little supplicant is herself: "I cut her head off. I slit her throat. Still, I expect her to like me."

References

Ackroyd, P. (1995). *Blake*. Minerva Press, London.

ArtLyst (2012). https://www.artlyst.com/news/louise-bourgeois-love-affair-with-freudian-psychoanalysis/

Banville, J. (2017). *Kafka: The Early Years*. New York Review of Books, New York.

Burnham, D. L. (1996). Loss and the Reparative Capacity of Imagination: The Case of August Strindberg, *Contemporary Psychoanalysis*, 32: 115.

Capps, D. (2012). The Replacement Child: Solomonic Justice and the Sublimation of Sibling Envy, *American Imago*, 69(3): 385–400.

Feder, S. (1978). Gustav Mahler, Dying, *International Review of Psycho-Analysis*, 5: 125–148.

Friedman, S. M. (1999). Form and Content in Van Gogh's 'Crows over the Wheat Field', *Annual of Psychoanalysis*, 26: 259–267.

Glenn, J. (1986). Twinship Themes and Fantasies in the Work of Thornton Wilder, *Psychoanalytic Study of the Child*, 41: 627–651.

Hartman, J. J. (2008). Dali's Homage to Rothko: A Defense Against Fusion with the Victim, *Psychoanalytic Quarterly*, 77: 531–567.

Holmes, R. (2015). 'The Greatness of William Blake', *New Yorke Review of Books*.

Klein, M. C., & Klein, H. A. (1975). *Käthe Kollwitz: Life in Art*. New York: Schocken Books.

Kligerman, C. (1972). Panel on 'Creativity', *International Journal of Psychoanalysis*, 53: 21–30.

Miller, A. (2009). *The Untouched Key. Tracing Childhood Trauma in Creativity and Destructiveness,* Paperback, Anchor Books, New York.

O'Casey, S. (2011). *Autobiographies I: I Knock at the Door and Pictures in the Hallway.* Faber & Faber, London.

Pollock, G. H. (1978). On Siblings, Childhood Sibling Loss, and Creativity, *Annual of Psychoanalysis*, 6: 443–481.

Ravenal, D. M. (1995). Henri Matisse—Love as Art, *Annual of Psychoanalysis*, 23: 199–251.

Riviere, J. (1952). The Inner World in Ibsen's Master-Builder, *International Journal of Psycho-Analysis*, 33: 173–180.

Silver, D. (1983). The Dark Lady: Sibling Loss and Mourning in the Shakespearean Sonnets, *Psychoanalytic Inquiry*, 3(3): 513–527.

Stach, R. (2017). *Kafka: The Early Years*, translated from the German by Shelley Frisch, Princeton, NJ: Princeton University Press.

Wanamaker, M. C. (1993). 'The Dread Voice is Past': Death and Guilt in Milton's *Lycidas, Psychoanalytic Review,* 80(4): 583–601.

Williams, M. Harris (2010). http://www.artlit.info/pdfs/Bourgeois.pdf

Wilson, E. (1988). Stendhal as a Replacement Child: The Theme of the Dead Child in Stendhal's Writings, *Psychoanalytic Inquiry*, 8: 108–133.

Postscript

As I complete this book, with the hope that the effects of sibling loss, especially when linked with an infant's devastating experience of the 'dead mother', may become better understood, Vladimir Putin has just launched his invasion of Ukraine. It seems important to say that Putin, as well as Hitler and Napoleon III, was a replacement child.

Many children, throughout the ages, have lost siblings. Families deal with it in different ways. Being a replacement child does not itself make one a Hitler. How a child deals with early trauma depends on innate factors as well as external circumstances. In this book, I have focussed quite narrowly on the sibling loss of particularly bright children who had an exceptional memory, an active imagination and who were full of fear and guilt that they could not explain. Their intelligence and wish to understand, as well as their capacity for love and humour, and extraordinary poetic sensibility, elicited love from others and sustained them. Many replacement children channel their experience into creative expression. Freud could devote himself to a life of trying to understand. The effects of being a replacement child play out in many ways including survivor guilt, being the illegitimate one or the 'special' one, not belonging, being to blame, intense unexplained paranoia and persecution.

Hitler was a fivefold replacement child: three of his siblings died before he was born, and two after his birth. He himself was a sickly child with an anxious and bereft mother. He tried to become an artist but failed.

Vladimir Putin was born in 1952 in severe poverty in Leningrad which had been under siege for 900 days and where more than a million people had died of starvation, many families entirely wiped out. His birth was preceded by the deaths of two brothers and he was seen as a 'miracle baby'. His teacher, Vera Dmitrievna Gurevich, said: 'By treating him as their "king", Putin's parents gave him a sense of entitlement—there's proof he feels chosen' (2000, First Person, *New York Times*).

At this worrying time in 2022, following the presidency of Donald Trump and the alarming surge of hate and anger in the world, it seems important for the psychoanalytic world to further explore the effects of sibling loss in early childhood.

Index

Note: *Italic* page numbers refer to figures.

Milton Keynes UK
Ingram Content Group UK Ltd.
UKHW021053300424
441963UK00009B/59